REFINED VISION
Monira Al Qadiri

REFINED VISION

Monira Al Qadiri

FOREWORD

Steven Matijcio

The Blaffer Art Museum at the University of Houston is honored to present the first solo museum exhibition by Monira Al Qadiri in the United States, which is truly an auspicious occasion for a young artist with a global reach that grows by the day. *Refined Vision* includes four newly commissioned works, thanks in large part to our generous and visionary partners at the Cynthia Woods Mitchell Center for the Arts, with whom we are proud to copresent Monira's interdisciplinary practice. The Mitchell Center supported Monira as a 2022 visiting artist in Houston, allowing for an extended engagement with our community and an inspired collaboration with Asia Society Texas. This catalogue is also part of the Mitchell Center's growing ambition to champion artists moving fluidly across disciplines and wrestling with the thorny relationship between energy, the environment, and what a sustainable future looks like. We are grateful to Adrienne Ropp and everyone on the Mitchell Family Foundation Board for believing in the generative energy that artists can bring to the University of Houston, and how they catalyze lasting connections between people, patrons, and organizations. Special thanks go to Melissa Noble, Managing Director, and Program Coordinator Sarah Jentsch of the Mitchell Center for their tireless work in coordinating the many logistics that such a project entails, and for being enthusiastic advocates of the impact this work has and will continue to have.

Monira's work is especially relevant in Texas due to her capacity and curiosity to illuminate a decades-long relationship between the Persian Gulf and the Gulf Coast as it courses through pipelines real and imagined. She dubs these societies "petrocultures," or petroleum-centric, in which the drilling and refinement of oil has shaped the ways in which resident cities have grown, developed, and behave. Exhibition curator Tyler Blackwell identified the potency of Monira's work to explore this network from a multidimensional perspective, and we owe him a special debt of gratitude for having initiated this project and steering it to fruition. Tyler has the prescient ability to find and elevate artists on the precipice of significant career growth, and his unflagging advocacy for artists previously confined to margins must be applauded often and again. His interview with Monira for this catalogue is refreshingly conversational, thoughtful, and sensitive to the personal cargo she has willfully embedded in the work. The larger dialogue between artist and curator as they shaped the exhibition checklist and tested the hypotheses of new works has produced a show that poignantly navigates a spectrum of emotions, memories, and meditations.

Refined Vision traverses the sublime that the oil industry has wrought in the world

Seismic Songs, 2022 (detail). Painted silicone, foam, microphone, video, sound.

today, from the otherworldly aura of refineries and the seductive spectacle of oil's effervescent sheen to the environmental damage and existential dread it inflicts. Oil's impact on climate change is a topic that escalates in urgency at every turn, but Monira's work has the unique capacity to temper necessary critique with a nuanced survey of just how pervasive petroleum circulates in all segments of life today. We cannot simply walk away from what she calls one of humanity's greatest discoveries and curses, and the crux of Monira's work resides in the autobiography she invests in this arena. *Refined Vision* is in many ways a self-portrait of an artist wrestling with the vivid, yet fluid legacies of her childhood in a rapidly transforming Kuwait; a country set aflame by war and greed. Monira invited scholar, writer, and curator Amin Alsaden to contribute an essay to this catalogue, and to confront the implications of her work from a similarly hybridized point of view. He does so in a manner that is personal, sincere, eloquent, and affecting —marrying critical distance with candid reflexivity. We are thankful for the thinking and memories they have shared, and their bravery to engage issues that go well beyond academic study.

Thanks also goes to the ever industrious staff at the Blaffer Art Museum who have made crucial contributions to realize *Refined Vision* and share it in an optimal way with our audiences. Youngmin Chung and Rob Kimberley overcame a variety of challenges and surprises to successfully install the exhibition and engineer strategies for works never before seen. Katherine Veneman orchestrated numerous partnerships to present a consistently captivating series of public programs; Colleen Maynard facilitated every contract with her signature warmth and grace; and Amanda Powers passed the design torch to AC Evans to jointly communicate the show with the dynamism it deserves. Blanca Wilson and her Security/Visitor Services staff never fail to humanize the visitor experience with charm and poise, and our team of docents have found a multitude of ways to connect students with the work. We are also grateful to Dean Andrew Davis, Assistant Dean Beckham Dossett, and all the employees of the College of the Arts for their continued leadership and council, as well as the Blaffer Art Museum Advisory Board for their unflagging encouragement and support.

We are pleased to continue working with Inventory Press on the design and production of this book, and we sing their praises as a leader in the field of art books today. A final—resounding —thank you to Monira who has brought all of these individuals and ideas together through her art, and kept us here with her courage, her disarming laugh, her modesty, and her ability to tell a stirring story with cinematic force and human affect.

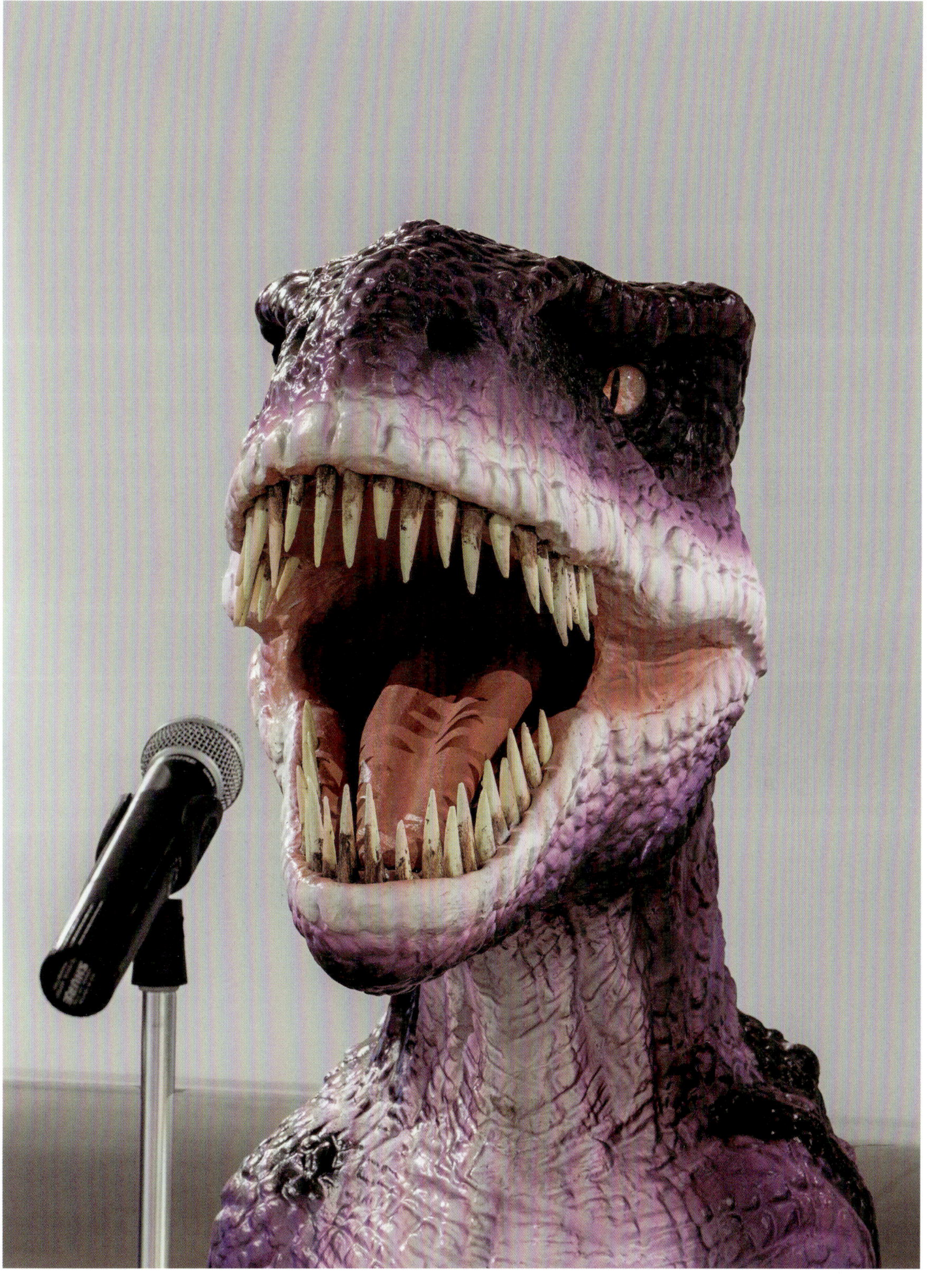

VISCOUS ENTANGLEMENTS

Amin Alsaden

On a few ominous days in late February 1991, Baghdad's clear winter sky turned black. Apocalyptic clouds, looming over large swathes of the region, were harbingers of one of the worst human-induced environmental disasters in history. After Iraq's invasion of Kuwait—an unprovoked aggression, in which a disagreement over oil production ostensibly played a major role—retreating Iraqi troops set ablaze numerous Kuwaiti oil fields. With the aim of hindering ground advancement and thwarting airstrikes, millions of barrels of oil were spilled into the Gulf, and more oil was burned to create a blanket of smoke that might obscure the land.

In Baghdad, where I grew up, the acidic rain left a layer of black residue, marking the rooflines of buildings with a craggy contour of soot. The morning after the rain stopped, earthworms, exterminated by the toxic water, covered the ground in nearby parks—one can only imagine what the oil poured into the Gulf did to marine species. But this is one of the lighter memories from those weeks, during which Iraq was pounded by fighter jets and long-distance missiles. We lived through unprecedented turmoil, even though the country had just emerged from a brutal eight-year war with Iran. We were under no illusion that the involvement of the United States and allied forces in the Gulf War was prompted solely by a sense of justice: the control of oil in this strategic part of the world was at the heart of what motivated global powers back then and continues to drive their policies and frequent interventions in Southwest Asia (or the "Middle East") today.

When I saw an early work by Monira Al Qadiri, *Behind the Sun* (2013), in which she revisits that same event from a Kuwaiti perspective, I was captivated. Those memories, like many others, are usually destined to disappear, just as that oil spill and the black rain that saturated the earth probably became a barely discernable layer in the region's geological strata. But Al Qadiri makes that event part of the world's collective memory through a deceptively simple work: found footage from 1991 memorializing the burning oil fields is juxtaposed against a contemporaneous poetry broadcast by Kuwait Television. The shaky visuals were shot by a driver who, approaching dark clouds that have turned day into night, arrives at a horrifying spectacle: everything, including the soil and trees, even the air, seems to be burning.

The voice-over—deep, masculine, with a rhetorical flourish—recites poems praising the divine sense of order evident in the harmony of the world. But the world on screen has been turned upside down. The orator highlights the heavenly balance seen in the earth's relationship to the other planets and the sun. Yet ironically, the artist depicts an inferno where the sky is occluded behind raging flames and vast plumes of smoke. There is something both terrifying and sublime in the imagery—and Al Qadiri clearly relishes sharing those scenes, which are undoubtedly part of the video's allure. The work is captured from the ground, invoking not only the experiences of Kuwaitis but the sense of awe that the artist experienced as a child witnessing the transfigured atmosphere. Al Qadiri is personally invested, channeling the way her community saw the fires and how they might have subsequently suppressed those memories, through devotion or distraction, perhaps as a way of coping with the traumas of war.

Al Qadiri brings that catastrophe back to public consciousness and raises important questions about humanity's detrimental impact on both land and air, through extractive capitalism, organized violence, the endless race to control energy resources, or deliberate acts of ecological sabotage. The video's continued relevance today is sadly all too evident, given the frequent environmental disasters and perpetual conflicts, as we inch toward the end of life as we know it. But the intimacy of Al Qadiri's work conveys a focus that is not solely confined to the global repercussions of our collective insatiable appetite for oil, or how that is accelerating climate change. Instead, her work seems more interested in assessing and representing—through a distinctive lyrical, whimsical, and at times even comical approach—how oil is inexorably enmeshed in our daily lives in more ways than we care to imagine.

For both Al Qadiri and myself, that surreal episode was an early encounter with the more sinister dimensions of oil, and a confrontation with how it impacts our communities in particular. We identified common interests in scrutinizing the global impact of oil, including the rapid modernization that transformed our region, the warfare triggered by the desire to control this vital resource, and the representations of Arab oil-producing countries and their peoples, especially by Western media and politicians. However, unlike other artists who have examined oil, from political, historical, and environmental perspectives, I came to appreciate the more unique aspects of Al Qadiri's work. While she denounces humanity's reliance on this substance, she thinks of oil as something integral to who she is, intrinsic to the formation of her identity. Oil for her is something that she cannot possibly escape or deny—and her work inadvertently implicates all of us in that reality.

Al Qadiri's practice has been invested in acknowledging that our global culture is fundamentally a petroculture, in that the material basis of modern societies is petroleum. This culture is so pervasive as to be insidiously normative, without us having the critical distance to clearly see our problematic dependency on the substance. Western democracies and their colonial expansion, along with modern nation-states worldwide, have been propelled by the oil extracted from Southwest Asia. Life is inconceivable without petroleum byproducts, or the petrochemicals that we obliviously consume, from domestic detergents to pharmaceutical drugs, from adhesives to paints to construction materials. We litter the ground with the detritus of oil-derived commodities like plastic packaging, we smother the atmosphere with smog emitted by the fuels that power our cars and factories, and we pollute our own bodies with microplastics. It is as though humanity has guzzled oil from the bowels of the earth only to create a new layer of human waste, to the extent that we now shamelessly have a name for the pernicious footprint we are leaving behind: the Anthropocene.

In the oil-wealthy nations of Southwest Asia more specifically, oil emerges from the ground, and soaks the land too—not just literally, as in the anecdote above, but, I would argue, culturally and experientially as well. For those of us who grew up or live in the region, there is a sharp awareness that we are on territories that produce oil. The industry's infrastructure—such as the refineries, with their recognizable forms—is a common sight, and our economies are so tethered to the global market for oil that we have become as familiar with its fluctuating price as we are with the weather forecast. In a war-ravaged country like Iraq, the use of oil is part of everyday life, particularly after the collapse of services following the devastating 2003 US-led invasion; people use products like kerosene, known colloquially simply as *naft* (Arabic for oil), for cooking and heating, or gasoline for the countless private generators that continue to supply power to those still deprived of mains electricity two decades after the occupation. In Kuwait, and other states in the Gulf, the ethos of incessant development is nationally acknowledged as an outcome of the oil boom—and it is not unusual for the post-oil era to be seen as coterminous with the age of modernity.

There is an intimate if seldom acknowledged relationship between the people, this substance, and the land in Southwest Asia—unlike in other places where my experience of oil became more abstract and distant, and perhaps where its presence is deliberately suppressed or concealed. This seeps into our language too. Etymologically, *naft* is thought to be derived from Aramaic or Old Persian, denoting petroleum or pitch, attesting to a familiarity with oil in this region since ancient times. But the same Arabic word, which has different possible pronunciations, also means to boil, to explode with rage, to sneeze, or to blister. These meanings allow us to understand oil as something that forcefully comes forth from the earth, erupting out of the ground with unknown, potentially violent, repercussions. There is something equally eruptive—I would say even disruptive—about the plurality of narratives, ideas, and meanings embedded in Al Qadiri's work.

Indeed, the profusion of subjects she touches upon can be as fecund—and as subtle—as the histories and implications of oil. In numerous sculptural works, such as *Alien Technology* (2014), Al Qadiri shares her fascination with the otherworldly beauty of the drill bits used to excavate the ground for oil. Some of her creations are monumental, others minuscule. Most are the size of precious ornaments that might be worn or placed on a mantelpiece—some have been displayed magically levitating above plinths. The surface of these polychromatic objects is akin to that of a pearl or an oil slick, iridescent, glistening in colorful reflections. Their mesmerizing skin contrasts sharply with their menacing forms: vicious prongs that evoke some unfamiliar weapon, parts of a futuristic device, or the severed tips of tentacles that might have come from a prehistoric underwater creature. Aside from her curiosity about the anatomy of the machinery that extracts oil, there is an emphasis on the unsettling, almost extraterrestrial, exoticism of these tools—which make our lifestyles possible but with which most of us are unfamiliar. It is a commentary on this alien-like, savage industry that has taken over the world during the past century, infiltrating the land, sinking its claws and fangs into all aspects of our contemporary existence. And yet its mechanisms of control, oppression, and annihilation remain just as enigmatic as those objects.

Al Qadiri also searches for links between the eras bifurcated by the discovery of oil. In the single-channel video *Diver* (2018), an ensemble of synchronized swimmers performs in a dark liquid, wearing dichroic purple bodysuits, with movements choreographed to a recording of a traditional song that accompanied pearl-diving journeys in Kuwait. The video loops and one gets the distinct impression of an entrapment, as though the swimmers—and all of us—are immersed, perhaps slowly drowning, in oil. In her attempt to connect with her ancestors, particularly the grandfather she never met who sang on a pearl-diving boat, Al Qadiri uses the lustrous color of a pearl, mirroring the shimmering surface of oil. Both colors meet in the swimmers' bodysuits, becoming a tenuous link, the spectral optics of which momentarily reveal a historical rupture. The fact that her grandfather is absent, even though he is at the center of this work, is uncanny, considering how, before oil, the trade in pearls was the foremost economic engine in Kuwait, valorized as the

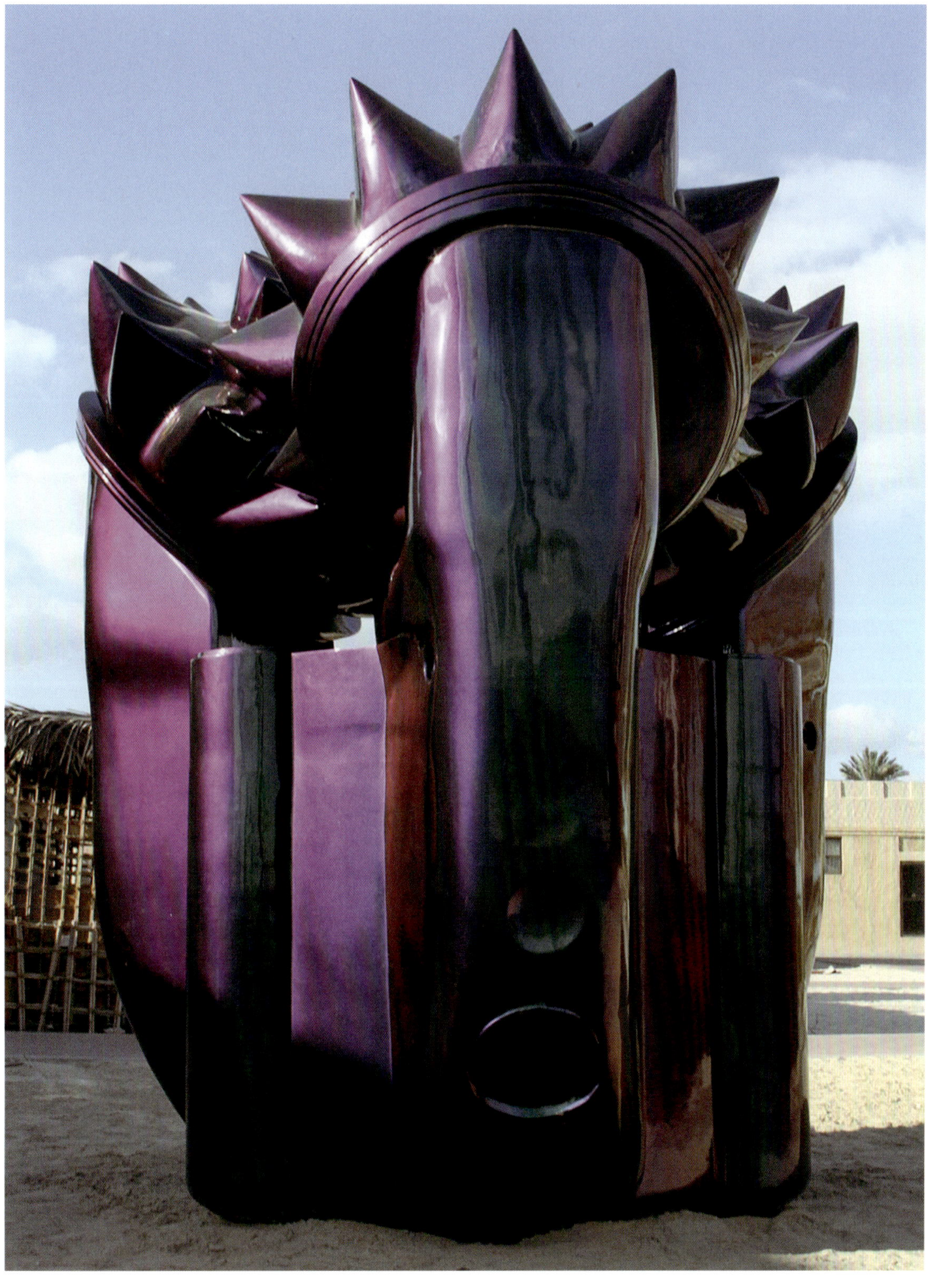

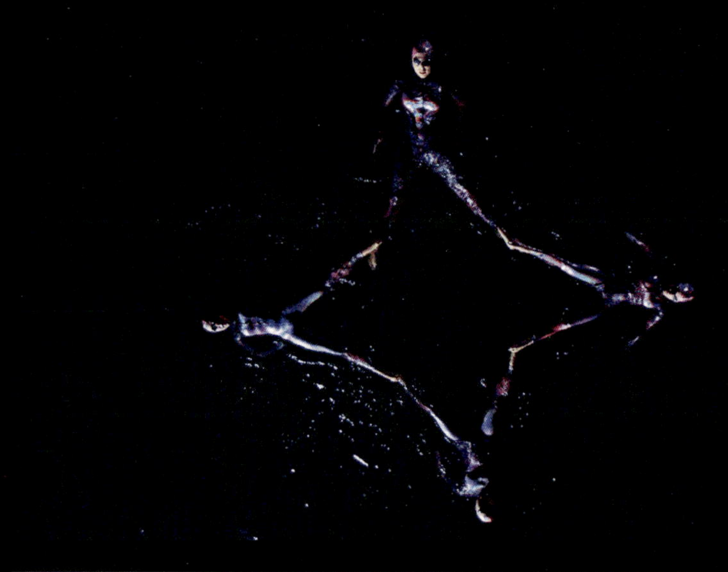

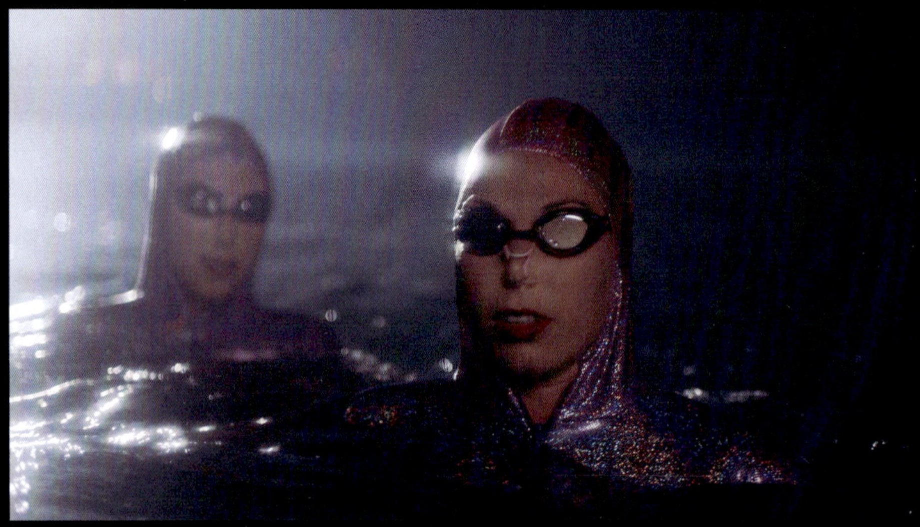

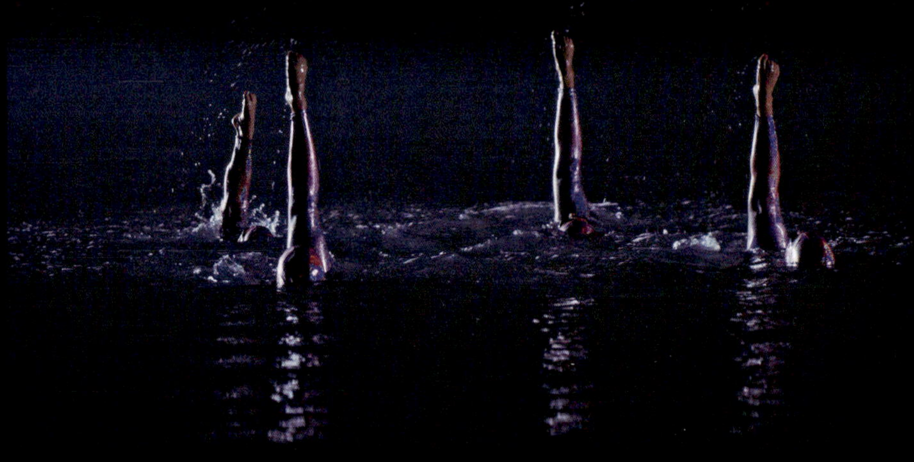

Stills from *Diver*,
2018. Video installa-
tion; 4-minute loop.

country's pre-oil, romanticized heritage. This withdrawal elicits the question of how society, rather than the state, perceives pre-oil times, and how its opulent modern petroculture overwhelms all other associations—oil is the starting point for everything, the beginning of time. These questions of visibility and cognizance are also crucial to how we understand or write histories of the nation, and the globe.

Moreover, *Diver* grapples with the question of gender, which Al Qadiri explores in several works. In Kuwait's patriarchal pre-oil society, pearl diving was dominated by men who were expected to have an exterior public life completely at odds with the domesticity to which women were bound. But the work also conjures some of the bizarre correlations, seen in the West too, between modern gender identities and specific domains. What is known as artistic (or synchronized) swimming is a relatively recent sport, traditionally exclusive to women, performed to mellifluous music. In this video, however, the swimmers at times seem to coordinate their movements with the guttural voices of men, who sing the pearl-diving song, and at others are out of sync—a dissonance emblematic of how gender itself is a social construct, performed according to certain codes. In other works, in which she cross-dresses or embodies male characters, Al Qadiri sheds light on these truths and challenges such codes, often by deploying humor.

In addition to questions of autobiography, gender, and national identity, Al Qadiri has also explored the intersections of land, mythology, and the legacies of colonialism. In the installation *Holy Quarter* (2020), what appear to be giant droplets of crude oil, strewn across the floor in a darkened space, serve as the foreground to a video projected onto a large freestanding screen. Upon closer inspection, the sculptural objects can also be perceived as strange organic matter, the sheen of their smooth skin reflecting the luminosity of the projection, revealing small protrusions on their variegated forms made of dark glass. On the screen, accompanied by eerie music, are shots of a mysterious, martian landscape, followed by the breathtaking dunes of the Empty Quarter—the desert in the south of the Arabian Peninsula—and finally, close-ups of peculiar natural formations. The video tells the story of a British explorer who was searching for the ruins of Wabar, an ancient city dubbed the "Atlantis of the Sands," but instead stumbled upon an impact crater, and the remains of a meteor, locally called Wabar "pearls." Wabar (also Ubar or Iram) was, according to legend, wiped out by God as a punishment. The voice-over narrates a fictionalized story of these pearls, as though the sculptures themselves are supernatural beings speaking in front of a documentation of their habitat.

Al Qadiri also alludes to regional narratives about the landscape of Oman, where the video was shot, rumored to be home for *jinn*, or genies, the invisible creatures familiar from Islamic theology. The work interrogates representations of our lands, often depicted by foreigners as an empty desert, connoting a terra nullius, thus justifying adventurous expeditions and military interventions couched in civilizing or developmental campaigns, but ultimately intent on controlling natural resources, like oil. For Al Qadiri, the desert is not only a fertile and elusive terrain but also the place where we might discover the earliest traces of life, and possible connections to the future and to a cosmos far beyond. She collapses time, place, and cultural references into one another, suggesting divine retribution as the response to an irresponsible and exploitative relationship to land. This resonates today more than ever before, with the ecological destruction that we are collectively—and callously—bringing about.

In their richness, layers, and even absurdity, to my mind these few examples are merely signposts, the beginnings of some of the threads that Al Qadiri has started weaving through her research-based practice and her long-term commitment to examining the manifold relationships between modern subjectivity—constructed individually as well as communally—the disappearance of traditional ways of life, humanity's relationship with natural landscapes and other creatures, the transnational demand for oil, unrelenting volatility in Southwest Asia, and planetary environmental degradation. These works are also inextricably linked with others where she has considered clashes between the past and new technologies, the region's penchant for tragedy, or gaps in the historical narrative, often due to the havoc wreaked by colonialism. There is an evasive fluidity and a staggering multiplicity to her practice, which mirror the immense complexity of the subjects she tackles.

Oil, for Al Qadiri, is replete with paradoxes. It is both an inexplicable miracle and an unspeakable curse; something extremely fragile which yet yields enormous power; a force capable of both sustaining and obliterating; a substance at once neutral and detached from humanity, but that is also deeply personal. Her work can be seen as an extensive, fragmented, and unfinished portrait of sorts, of herself and of our world—painting an image of a global petroculture that refuses to look at itself in the mirror. She is not ambivalent about oil, but hers is a nuanced perspective that accounts for both the good and evil, and probes everything in between, from the vantage point of someone with an idiosyncratic lived experience. Al Qadiri regards oil in all its pungent, opaque, raucous, bitter, and viscous entanglements.

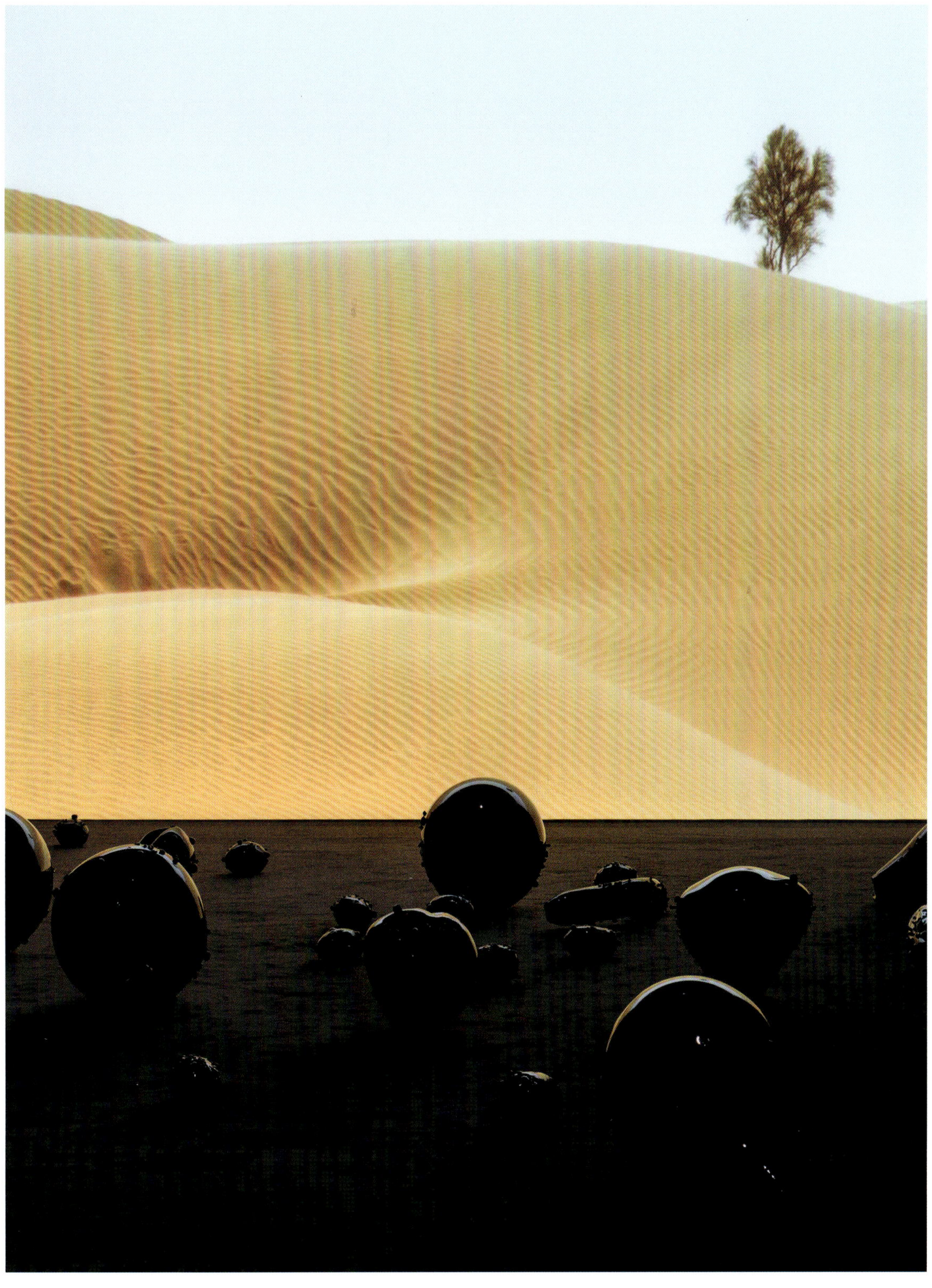

PLATES

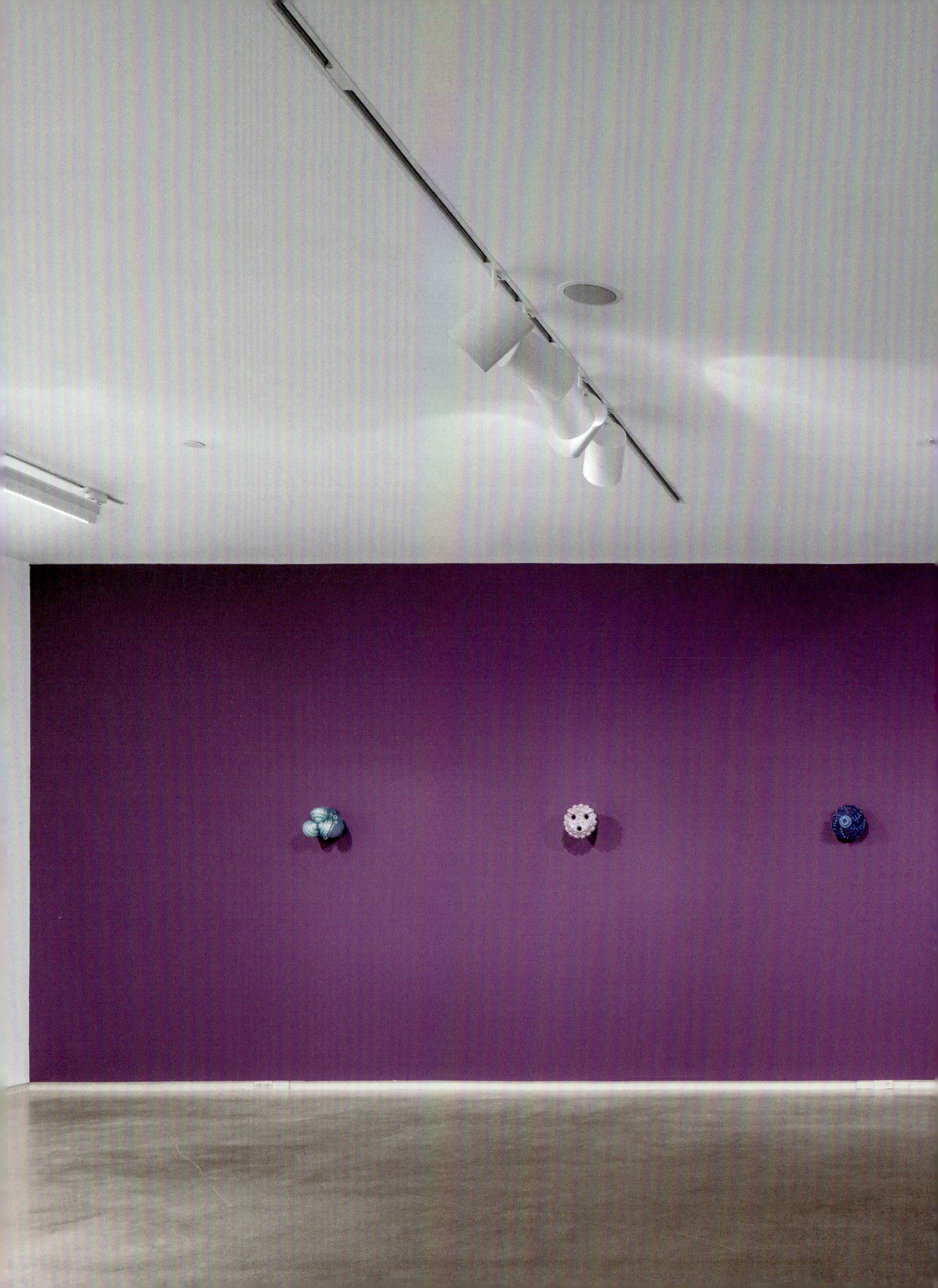

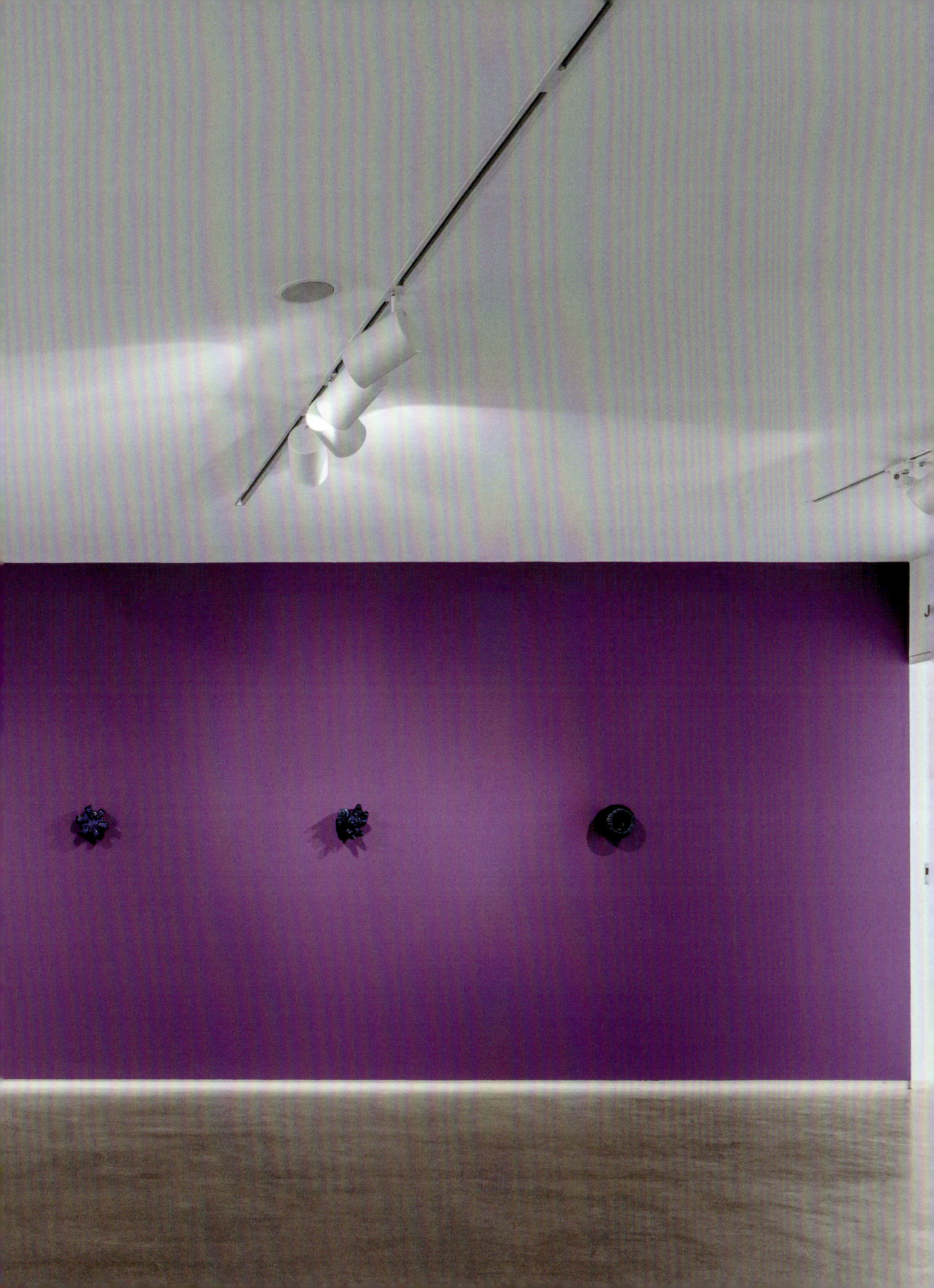

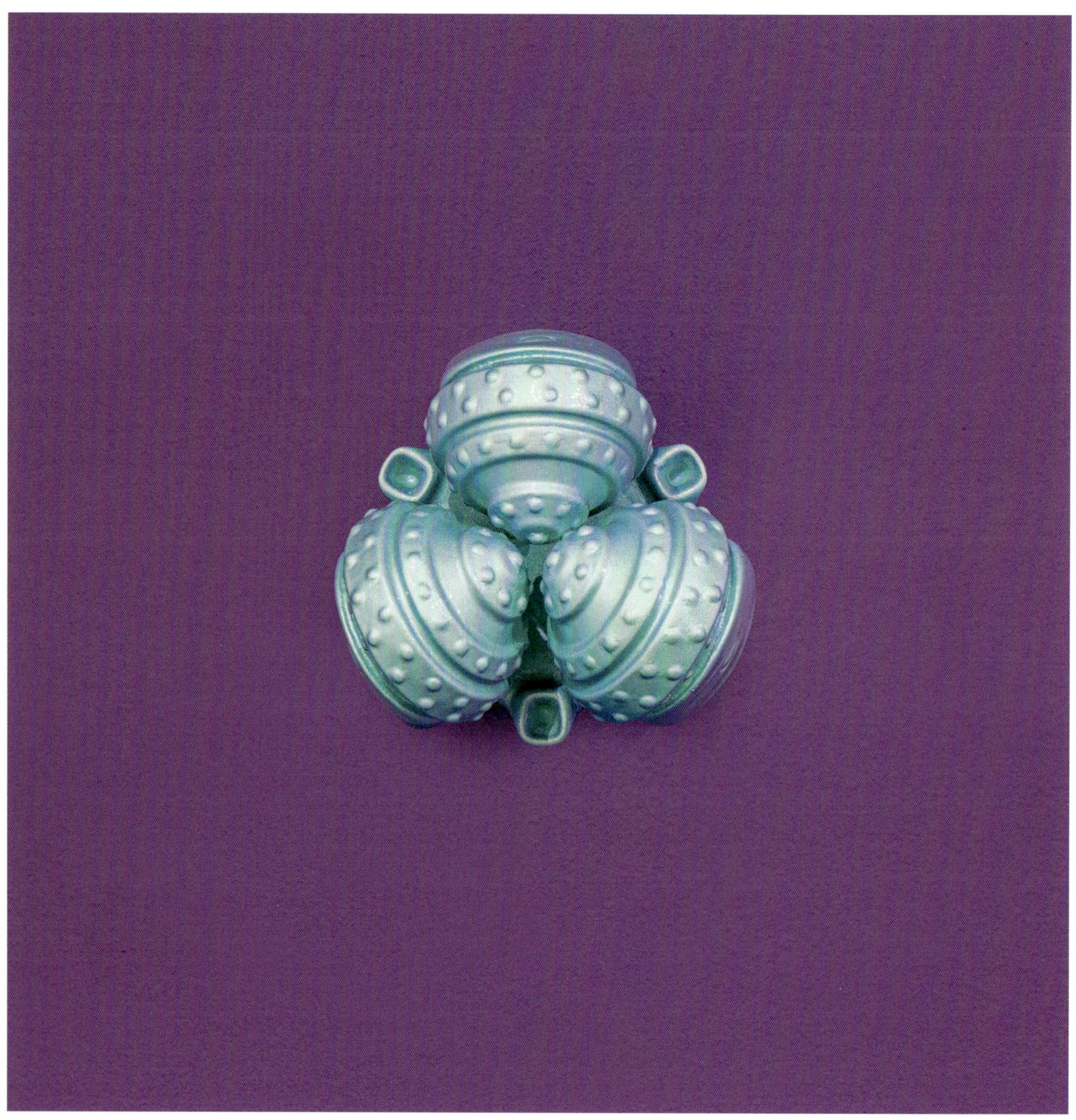

Previous spread:
Spectrum, 2016.
Installation view,
Monira Al Qadiri:
Refined Vision,
Blaffer Art Museum.
Six 3D-printed
sculptures, auto-
motive paint;
dimensions variable.

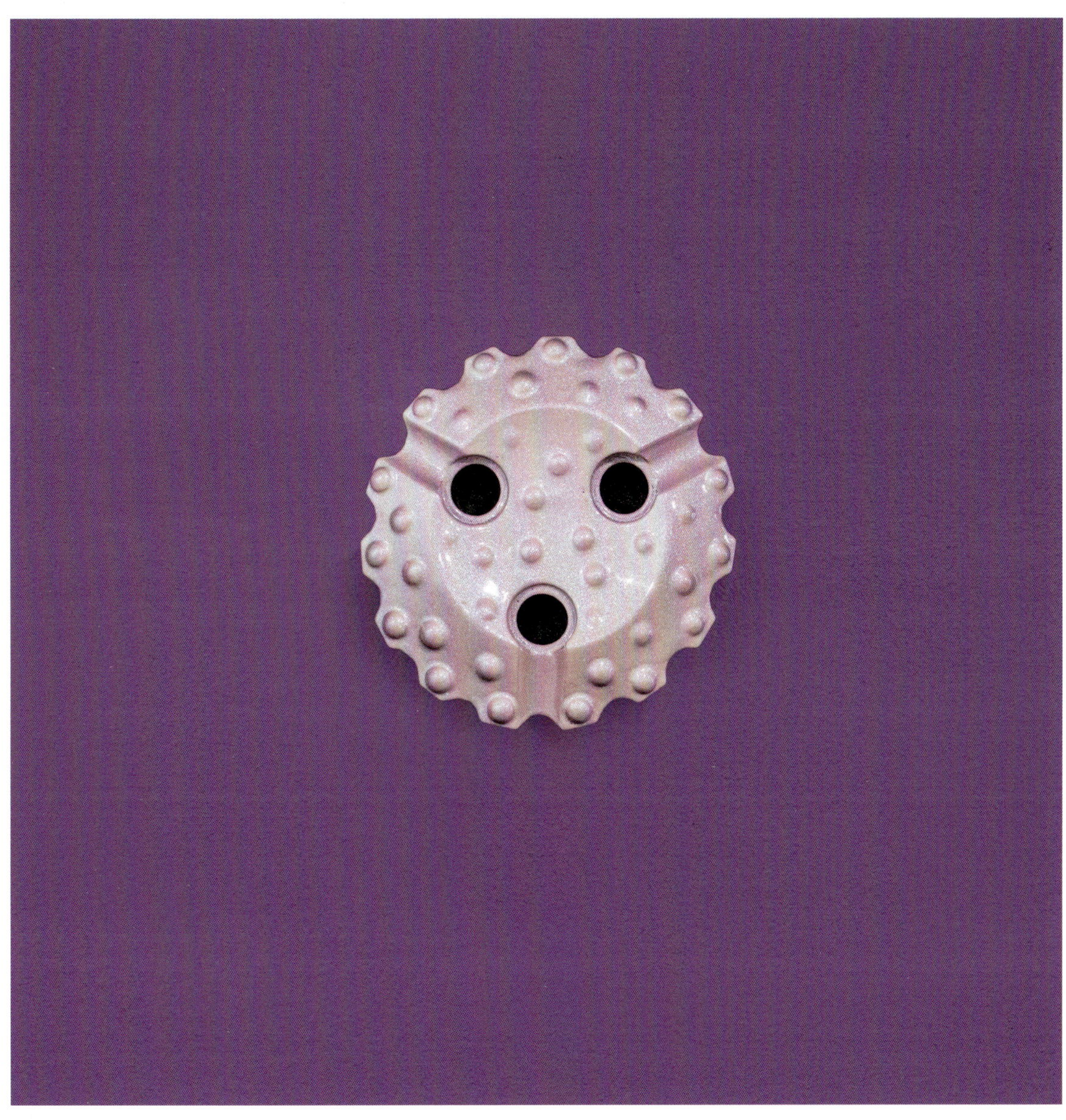

Above and opposite:
Spectrum, 2016
(detail, installed).
Six 3D-printed
sculptures, automo-
tive paint.

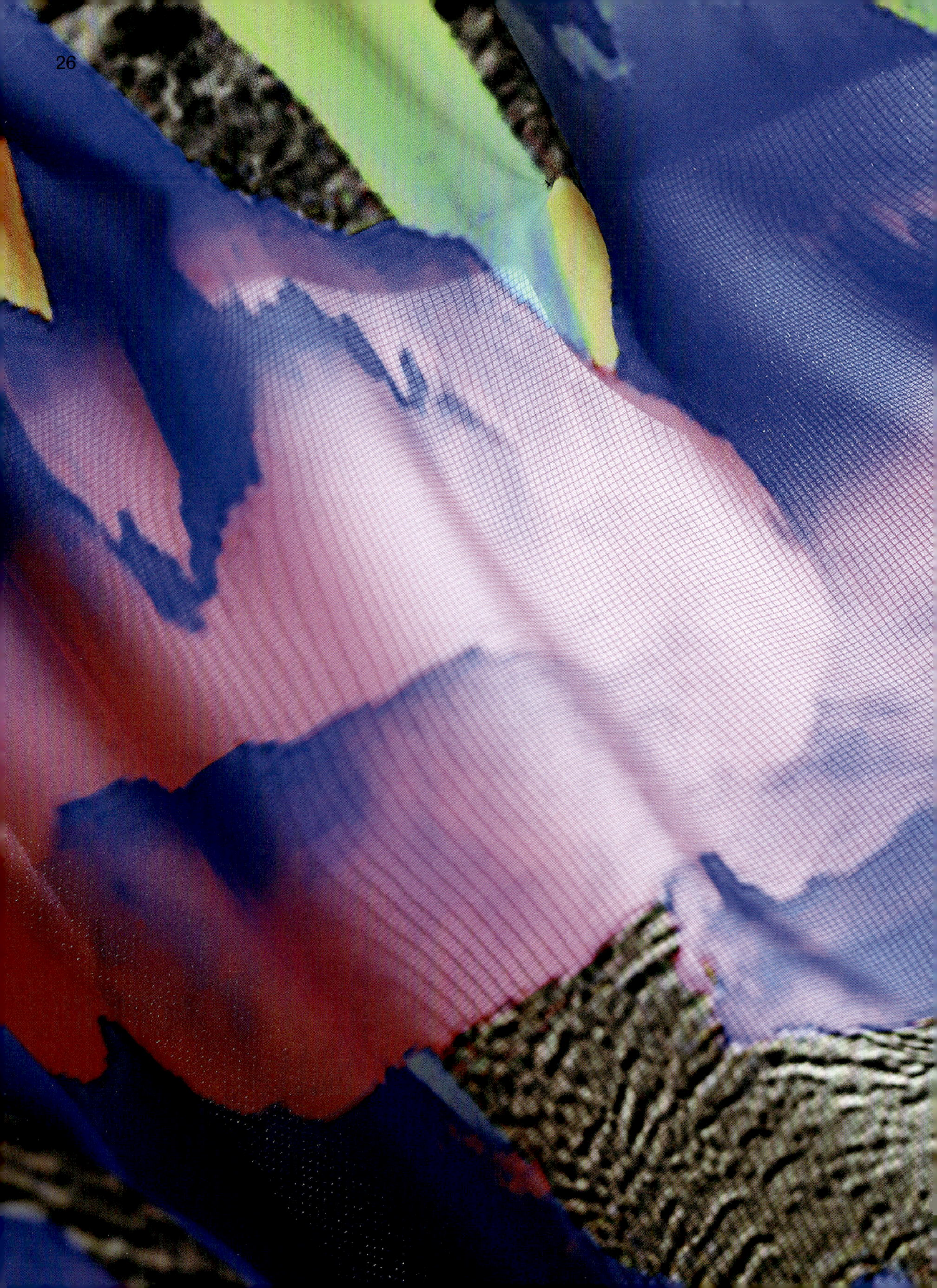

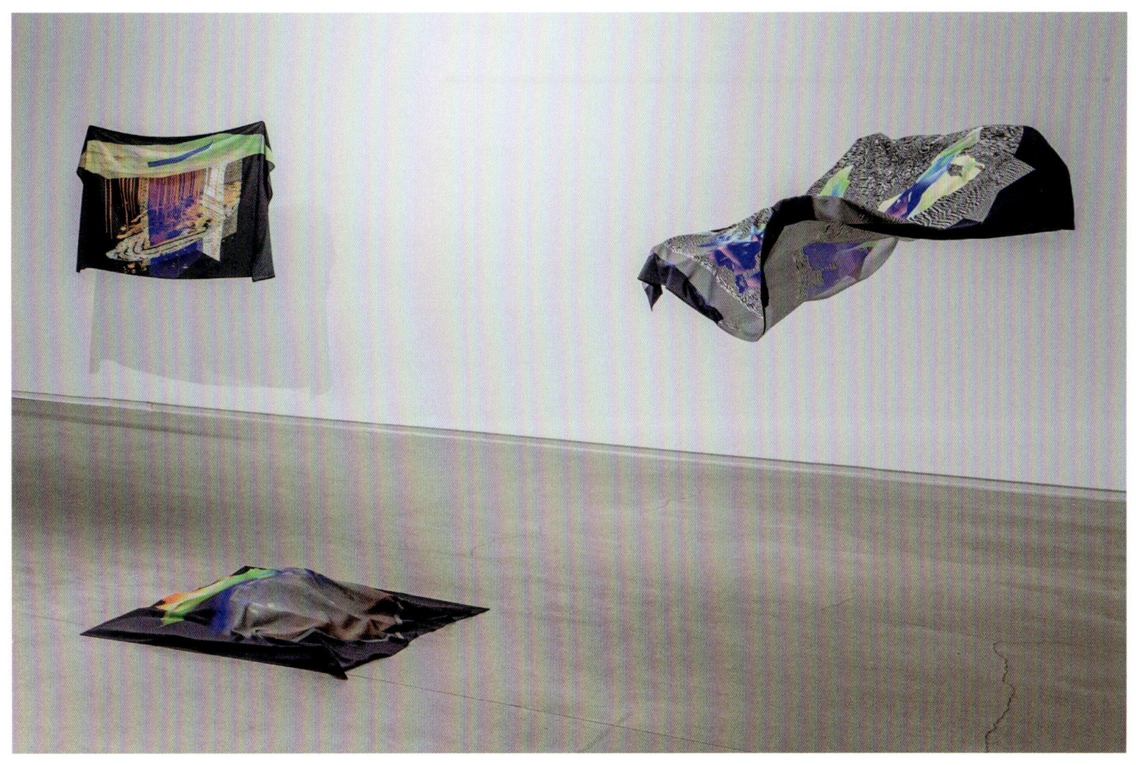

Opposite and above:
Reservoir, 2019.
Detail and installa-
tion view, *Monira
Al Qadiri: Refined
Vision*, Blaffer Art
Museum. Printed
fabrics and wire
grids; dimensions
variable.

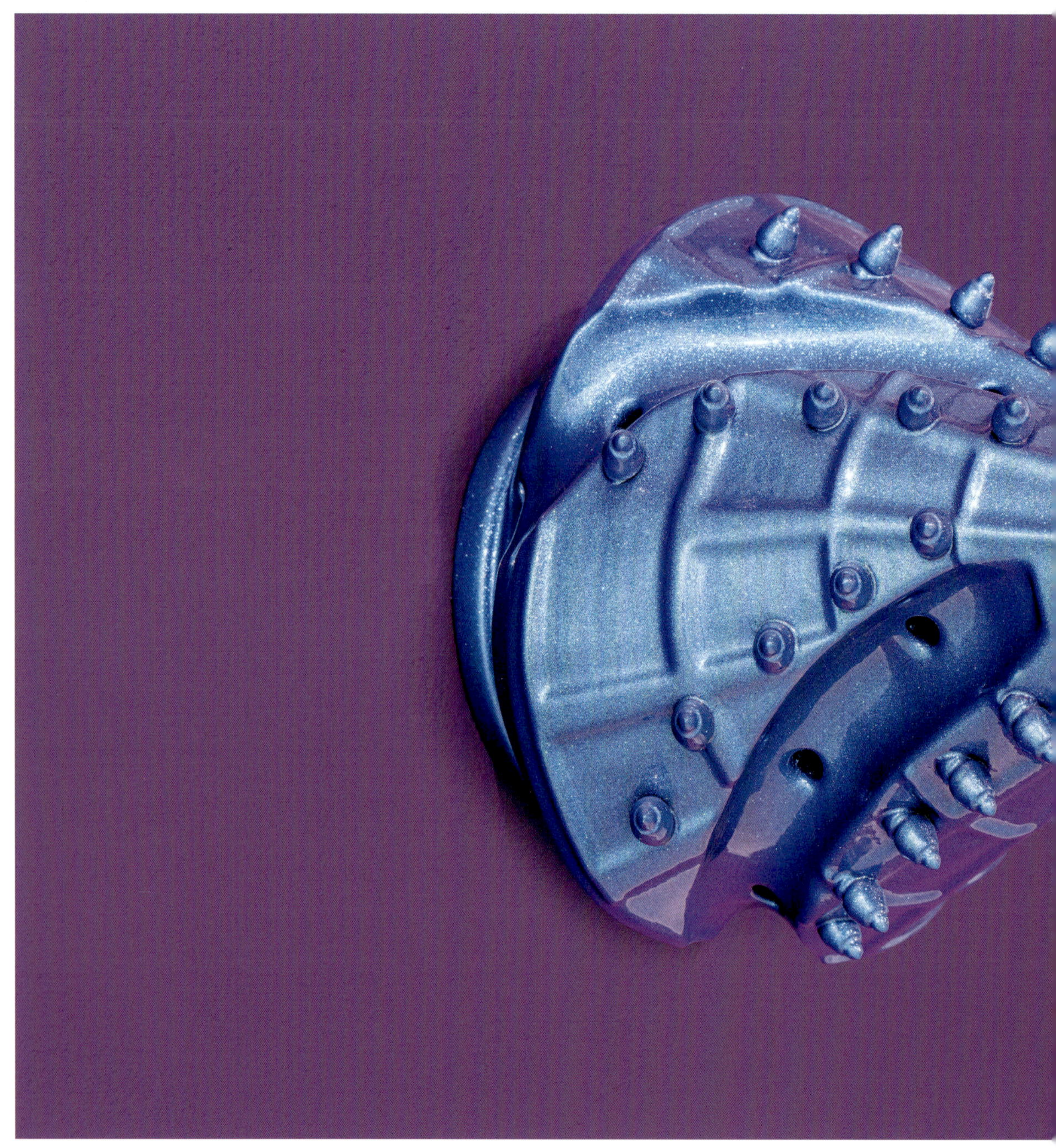

Spectrum, 2016
(detail, installed).
Six 3D-printed
sculptures, automo-
tive paint.

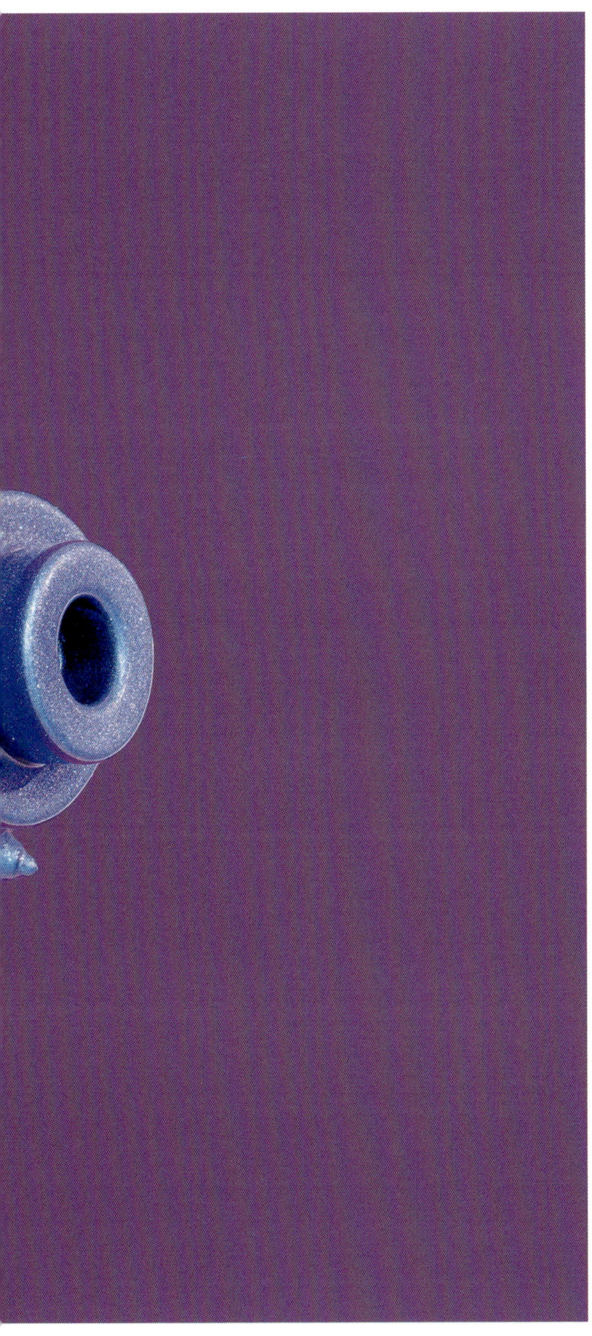

Next spread:
Installation view,
Monira Al Qadiri:
Refined Vision,
Blaffer Art Museum.

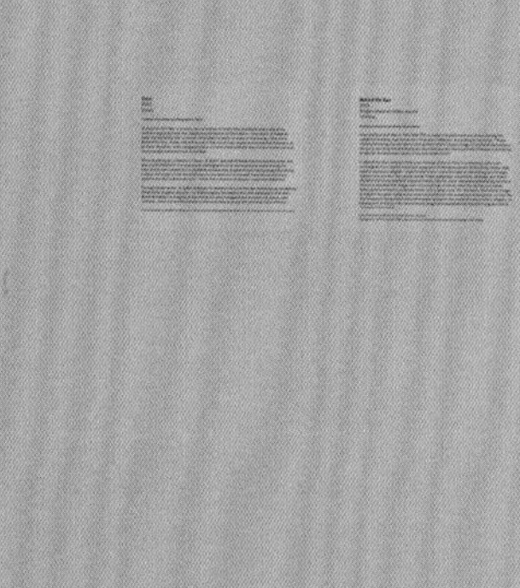
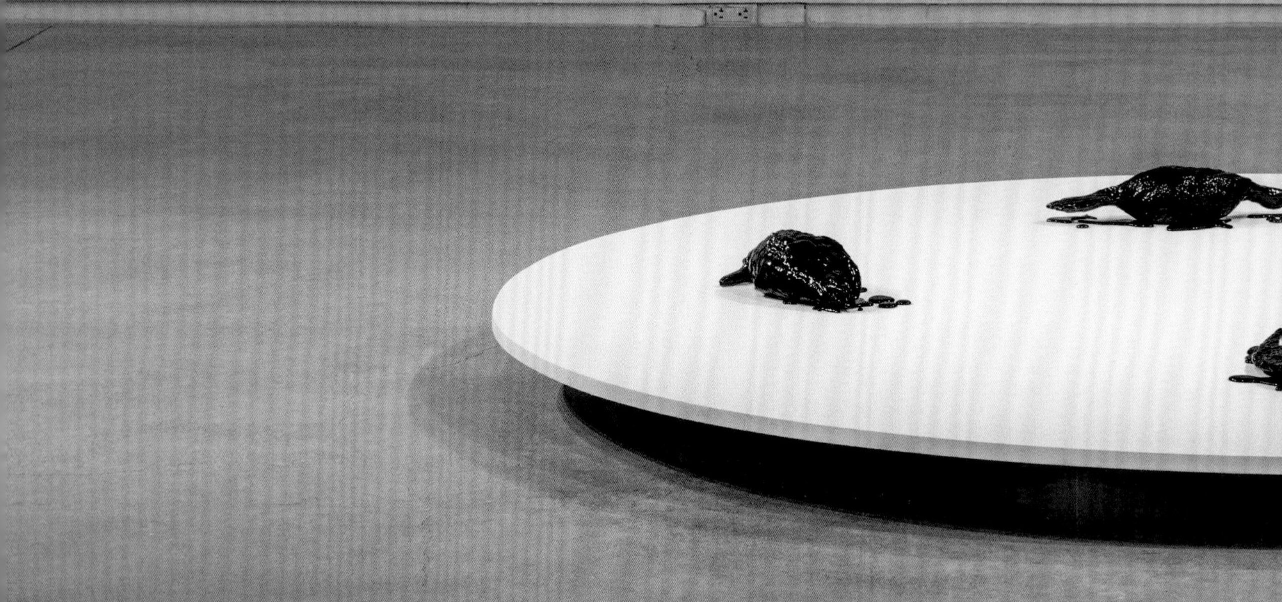

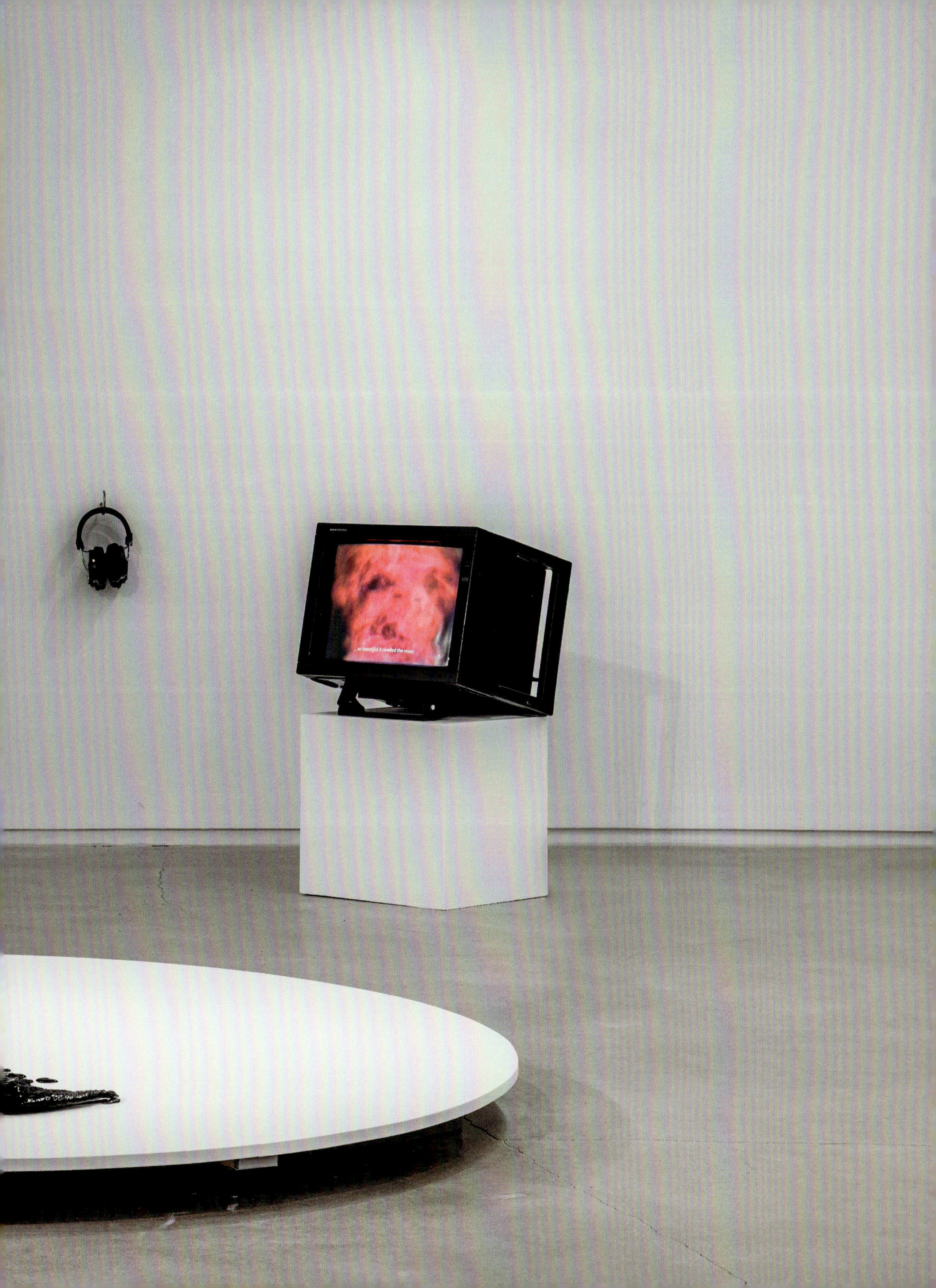

...so beautiful it rivalled the roses

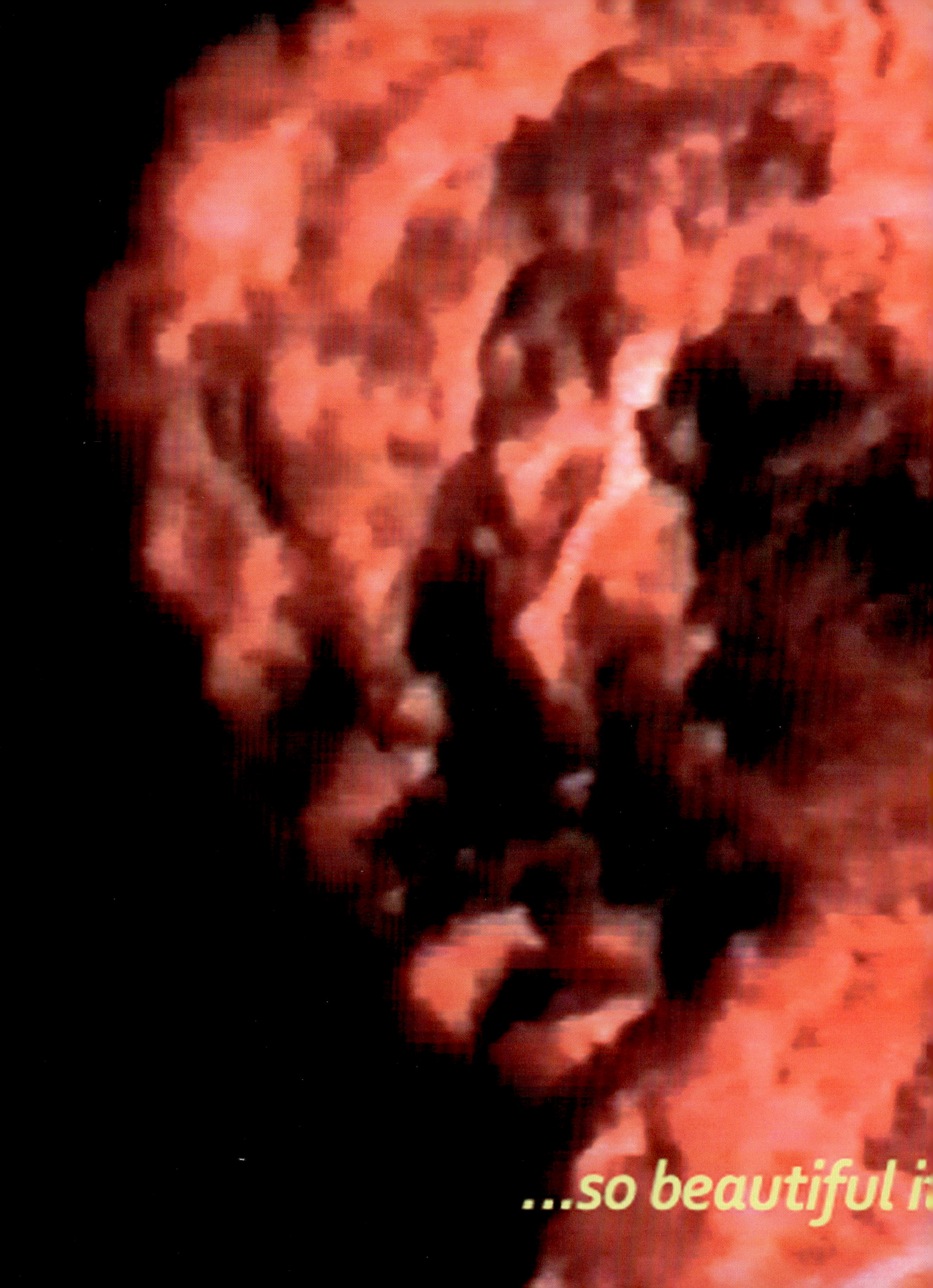
...so beautiful i

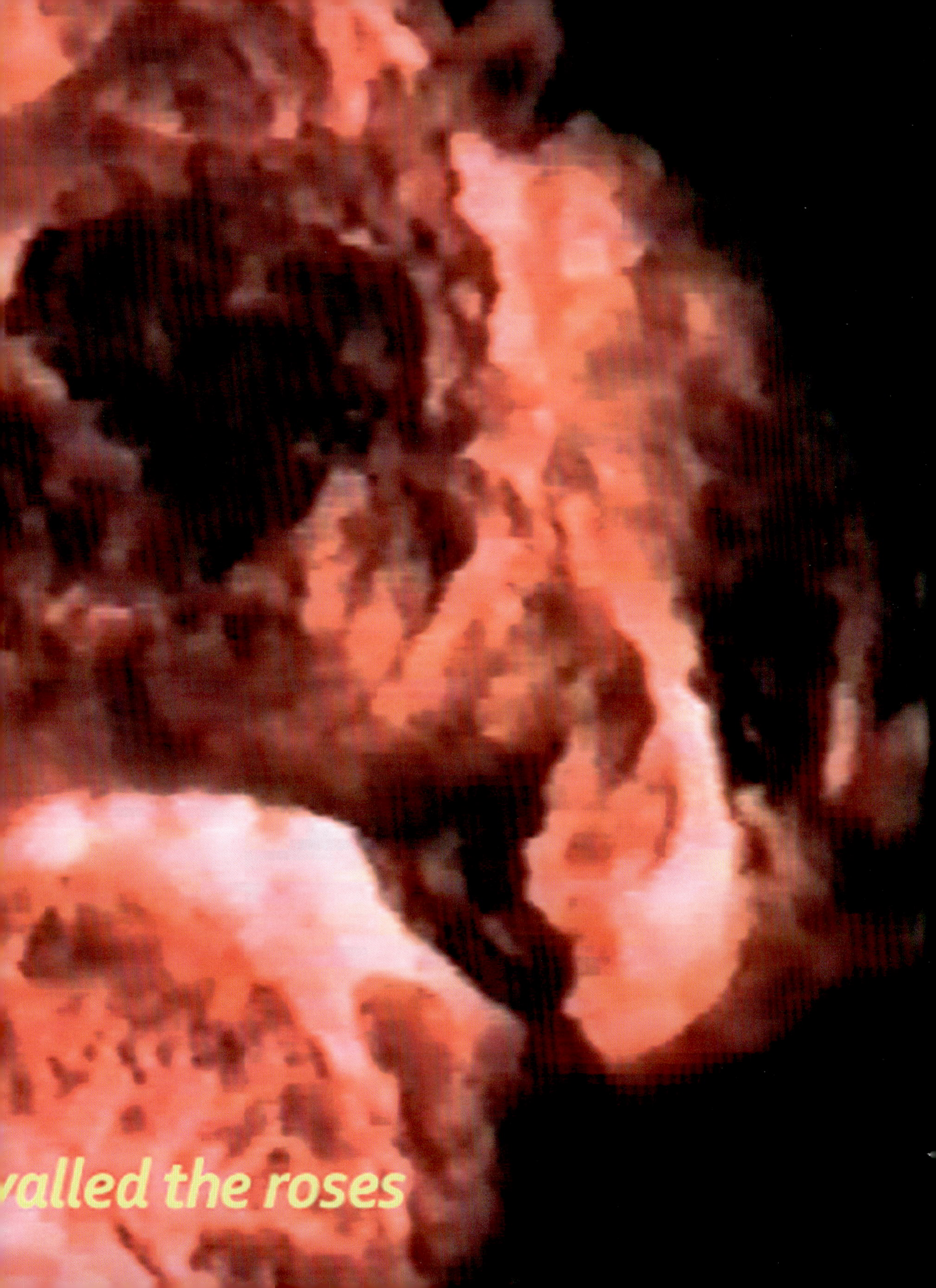
valled the roses

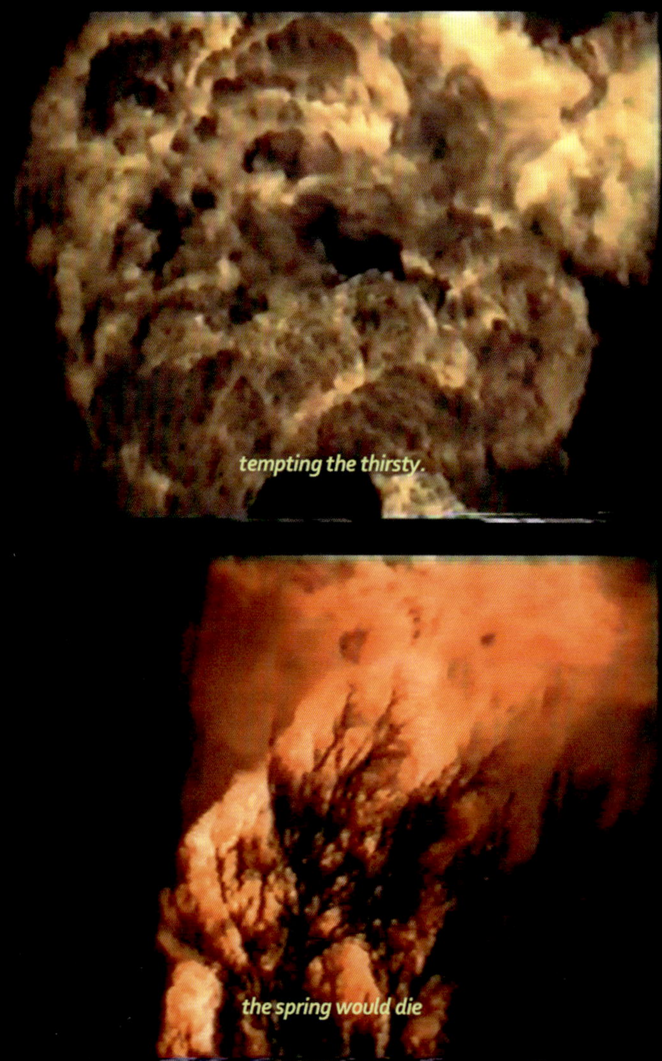

tempting the thirsty.

the spring would die

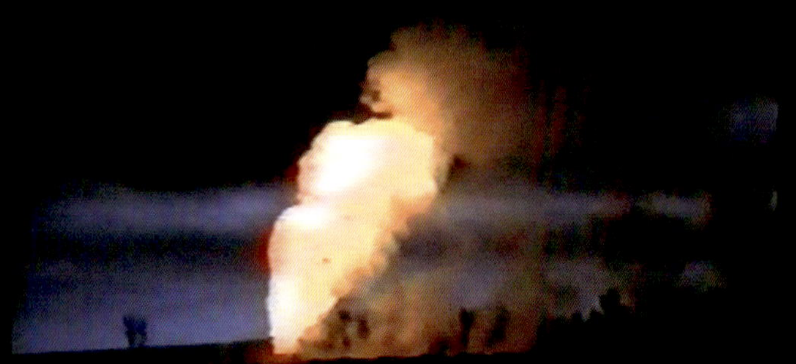

the sun's beauty shines unabated

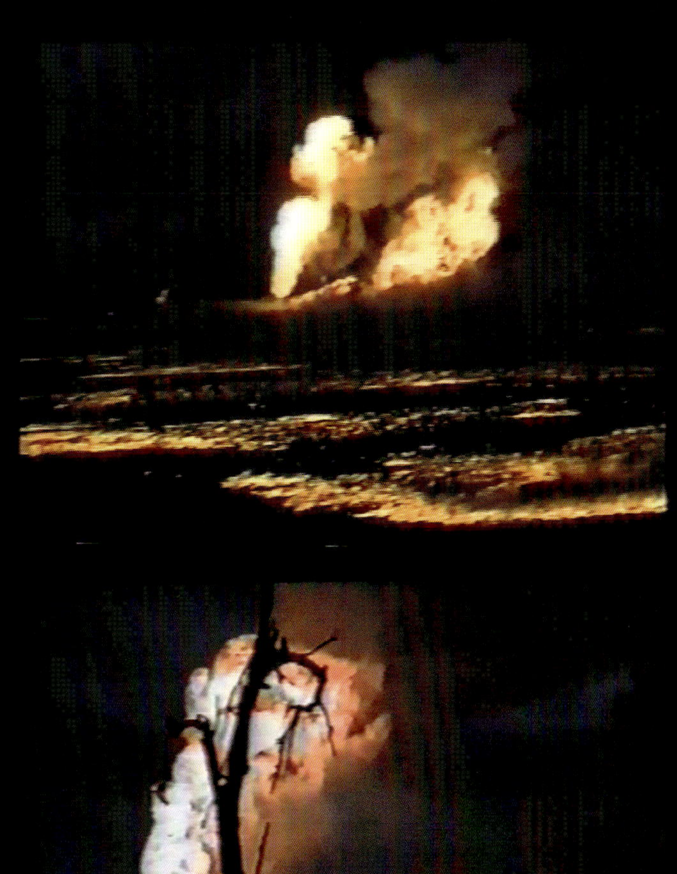

to answer the plea of His creation

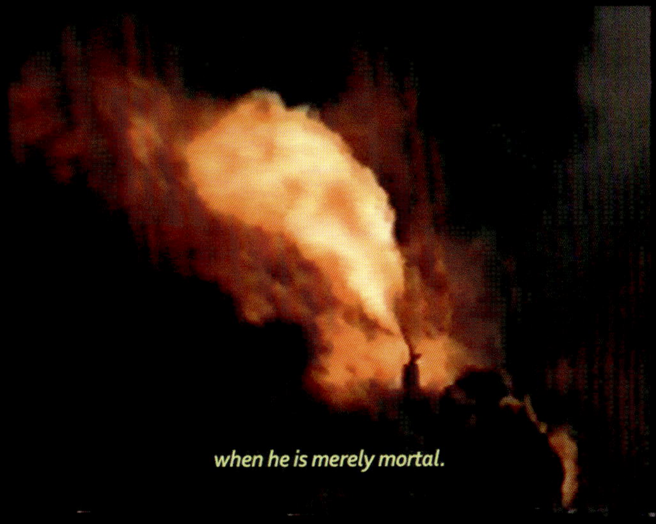

when he is merely mortal.

Previous two spreads:
Stills from *Behind the Sun*, 2013. Single-channel video; 10 minutes.

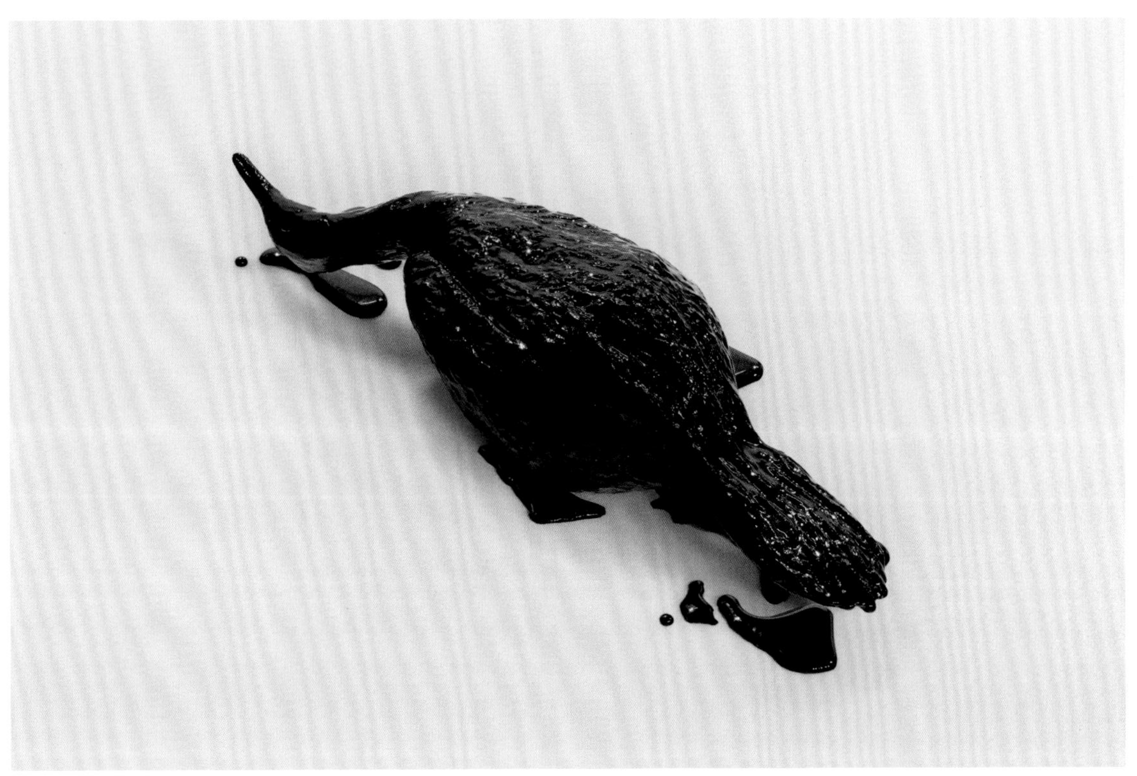

Above and next spread: *Onus*, 2022 (details). Cast glass; dimensions variable.

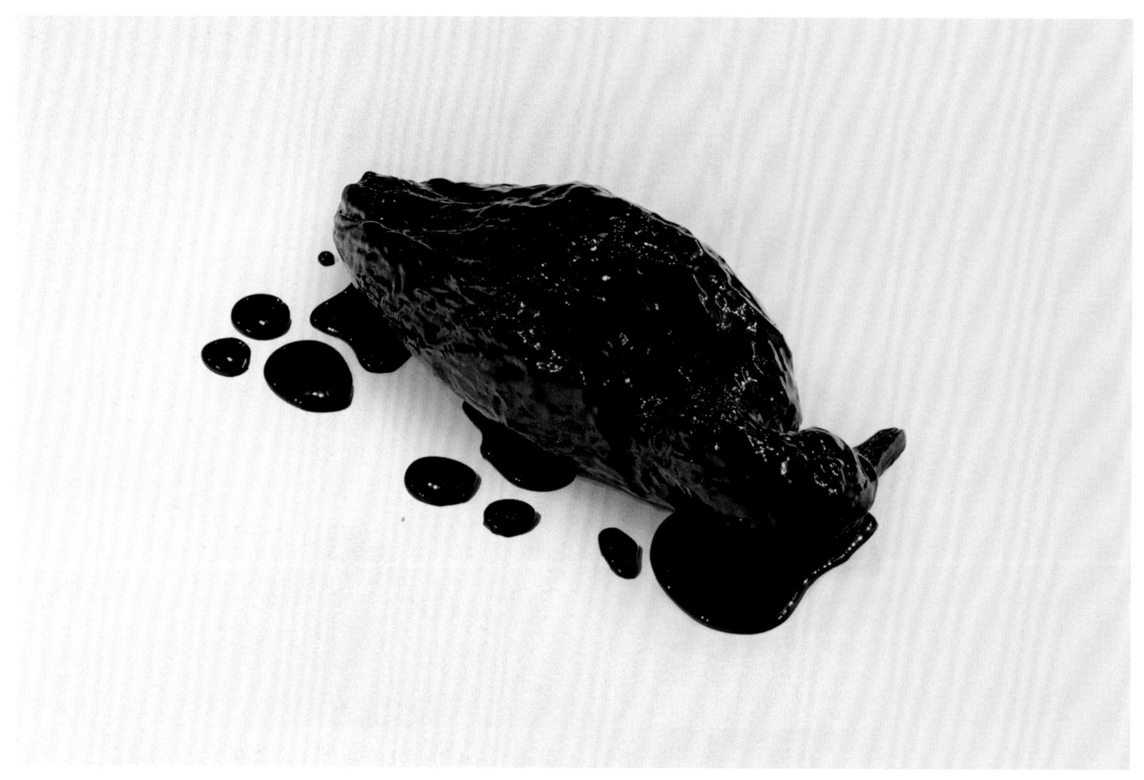

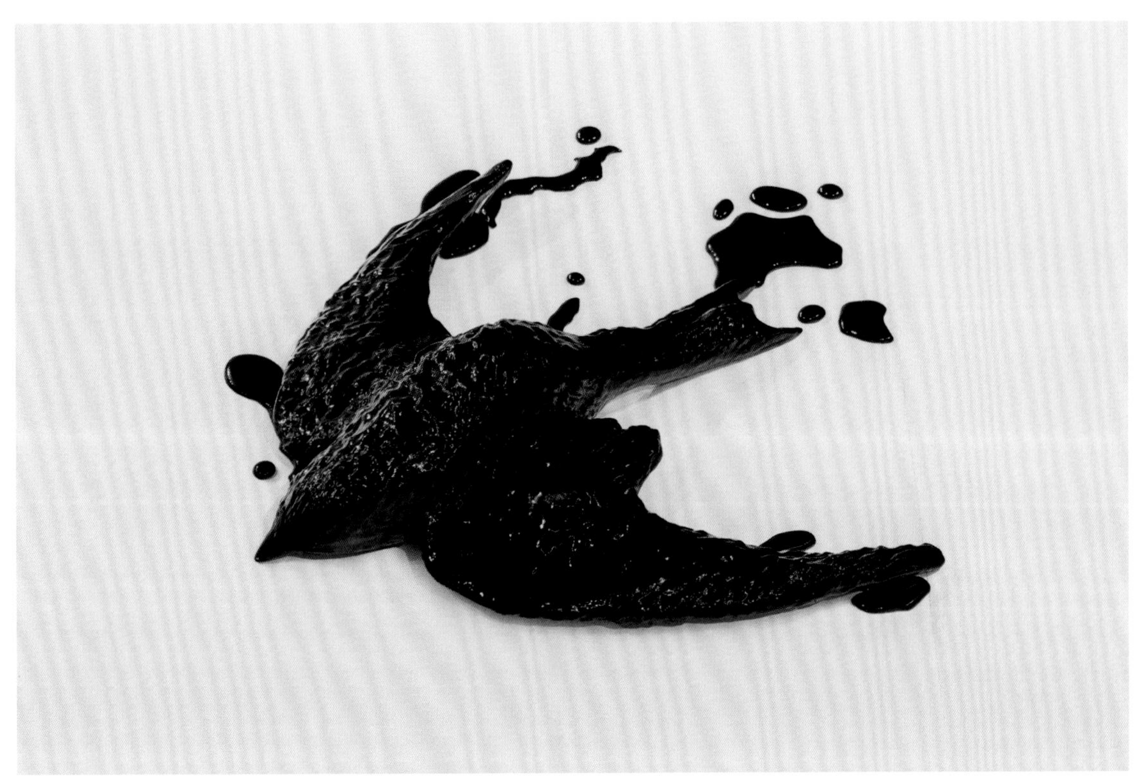

Reservoir, 2019
(detail). Printed fab-
rics and wire grids.

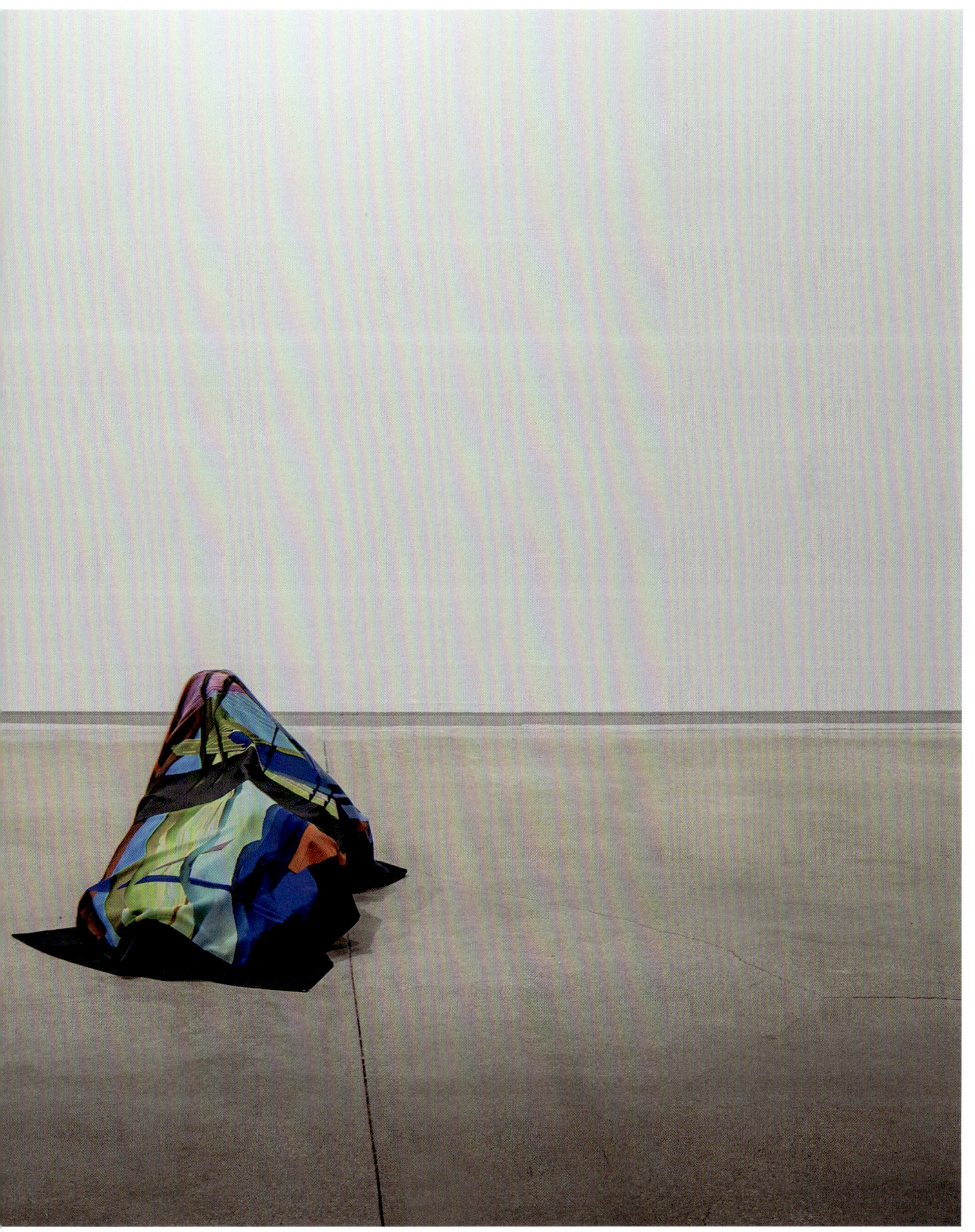

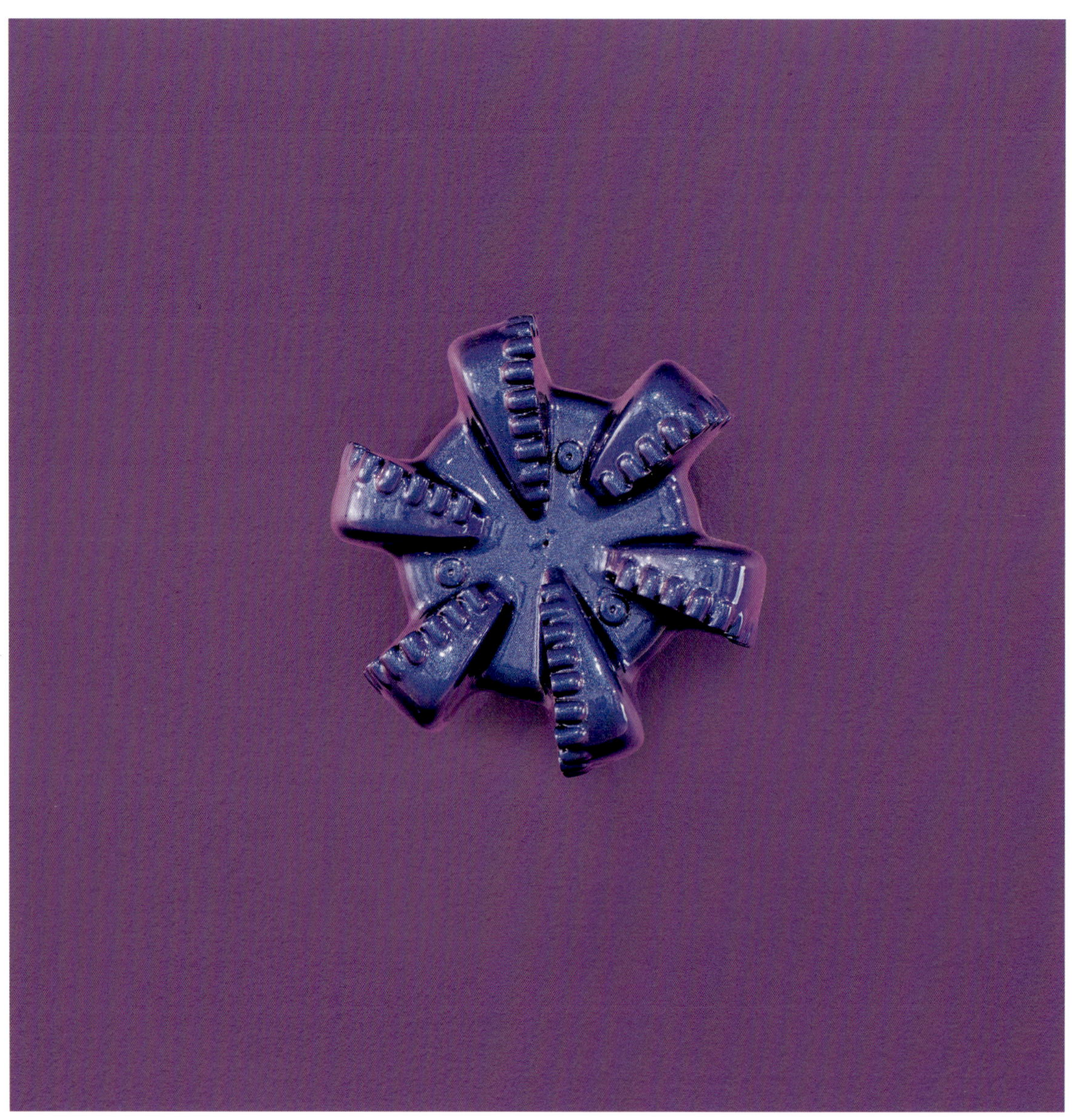

Above and opposite:
Spectrum, 2016
(details, installed).
Six 3D-printed
sculptures, automo-
tive paint.

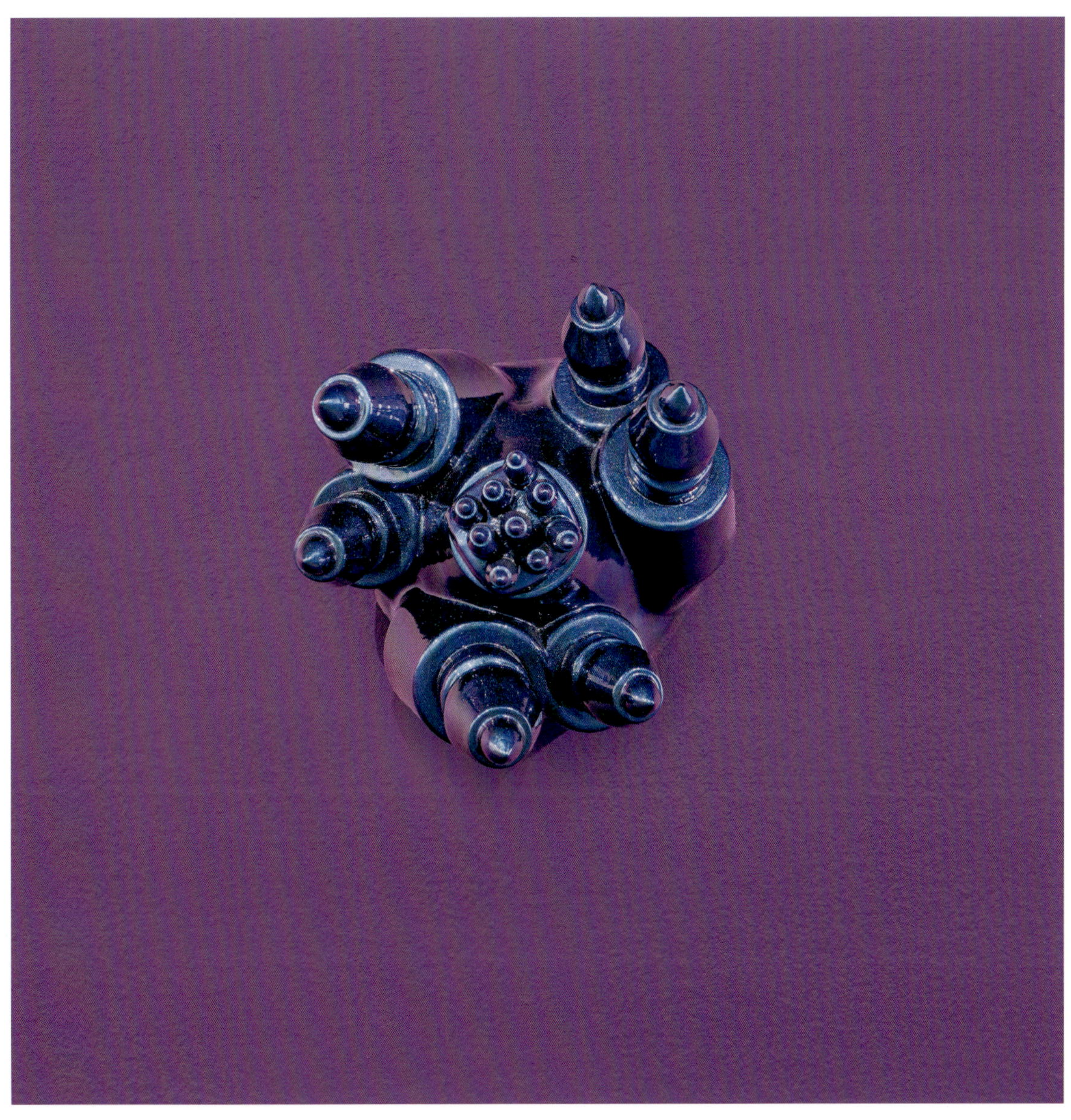

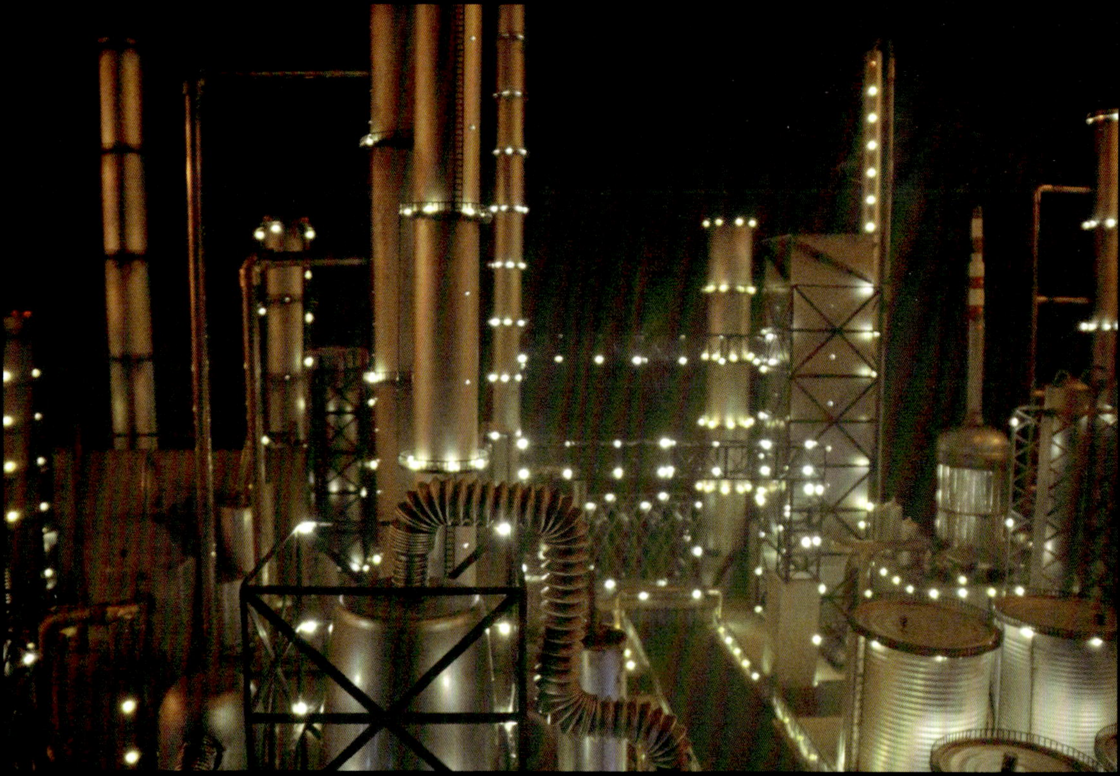

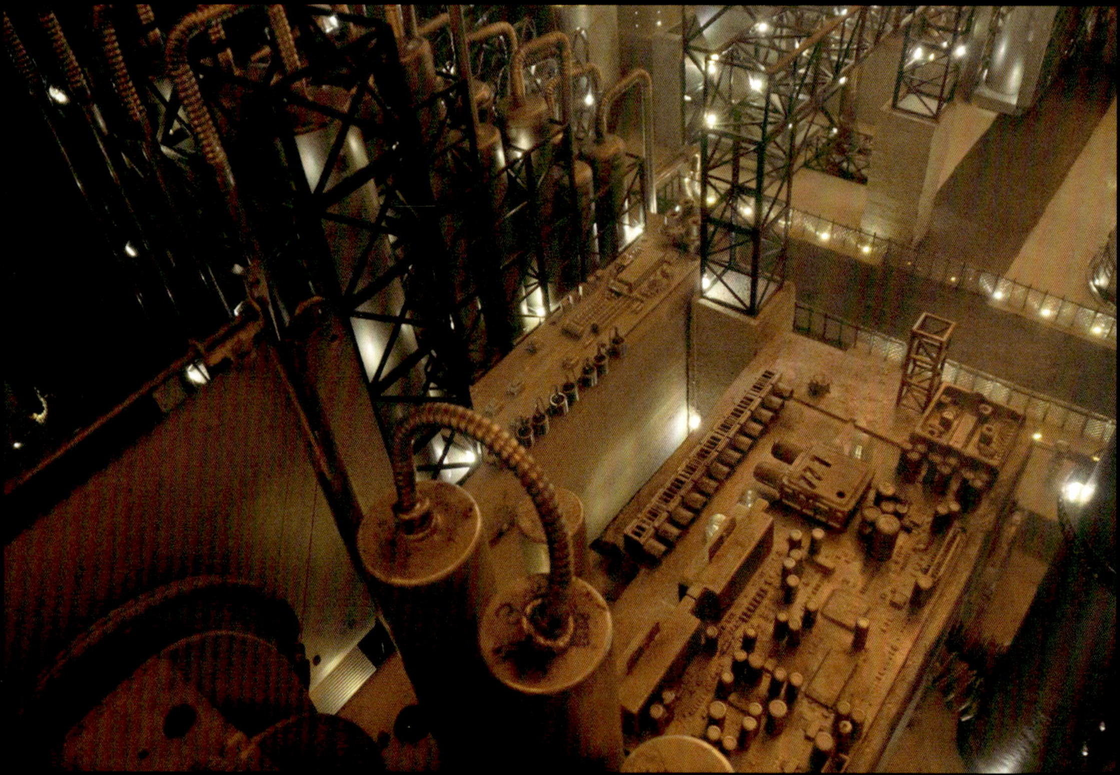

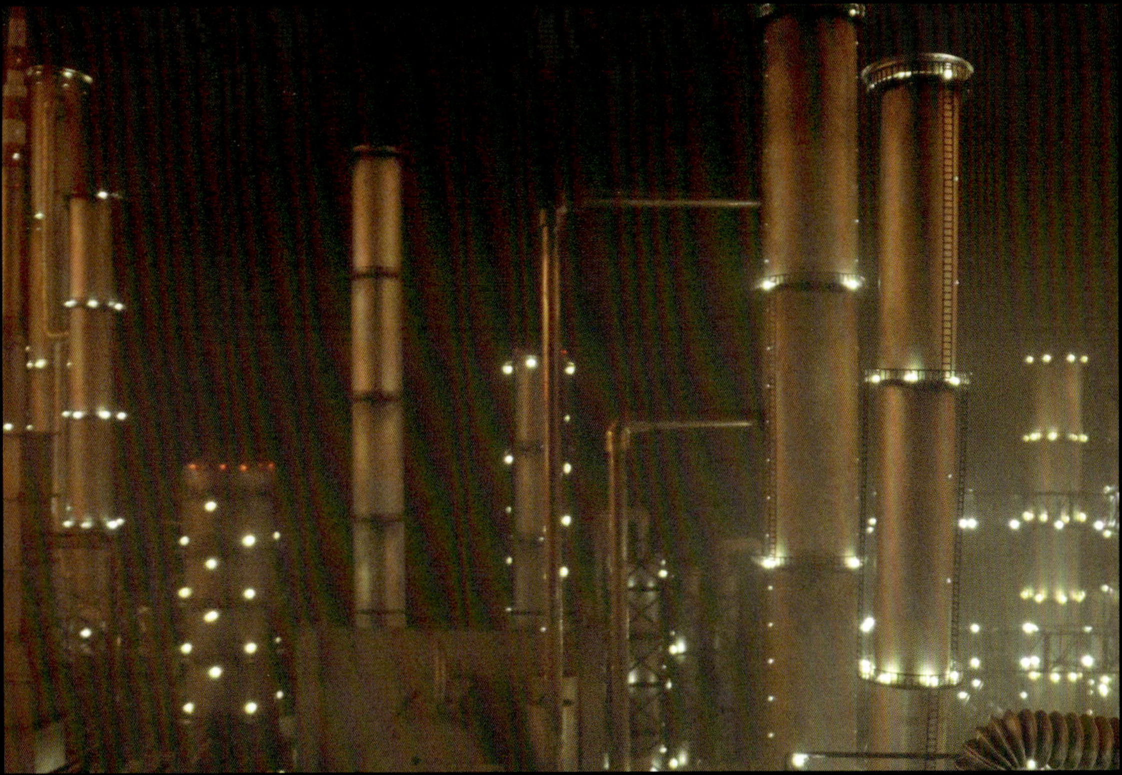

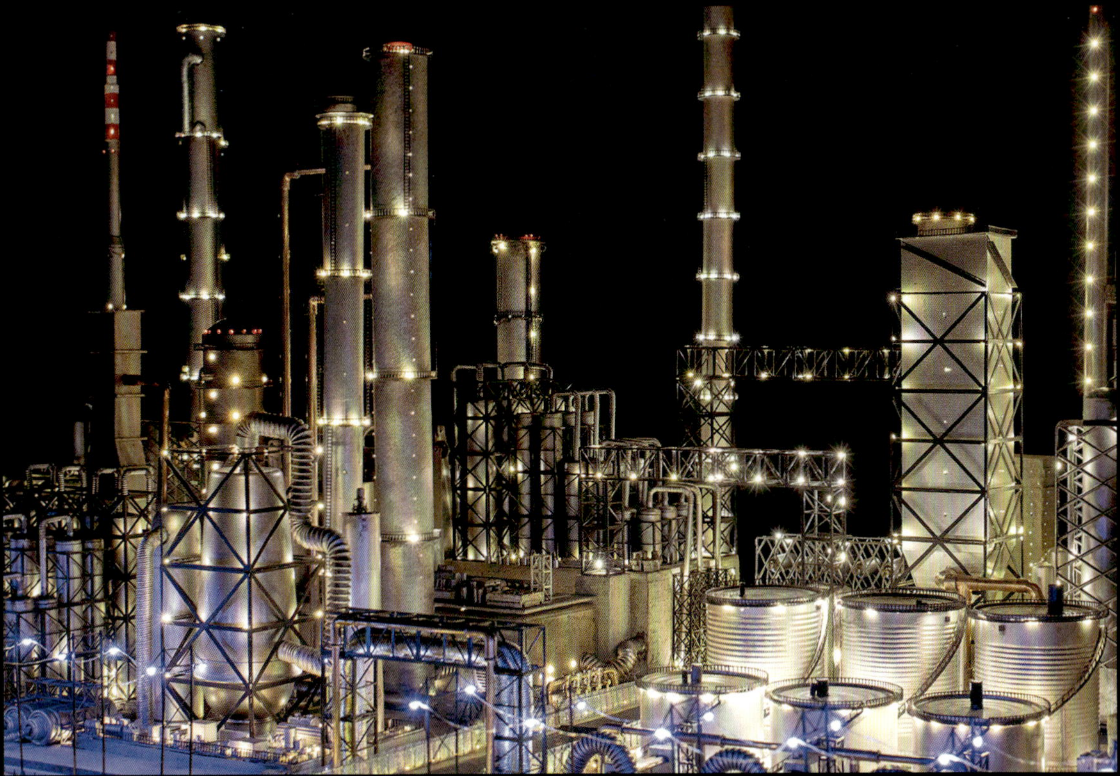

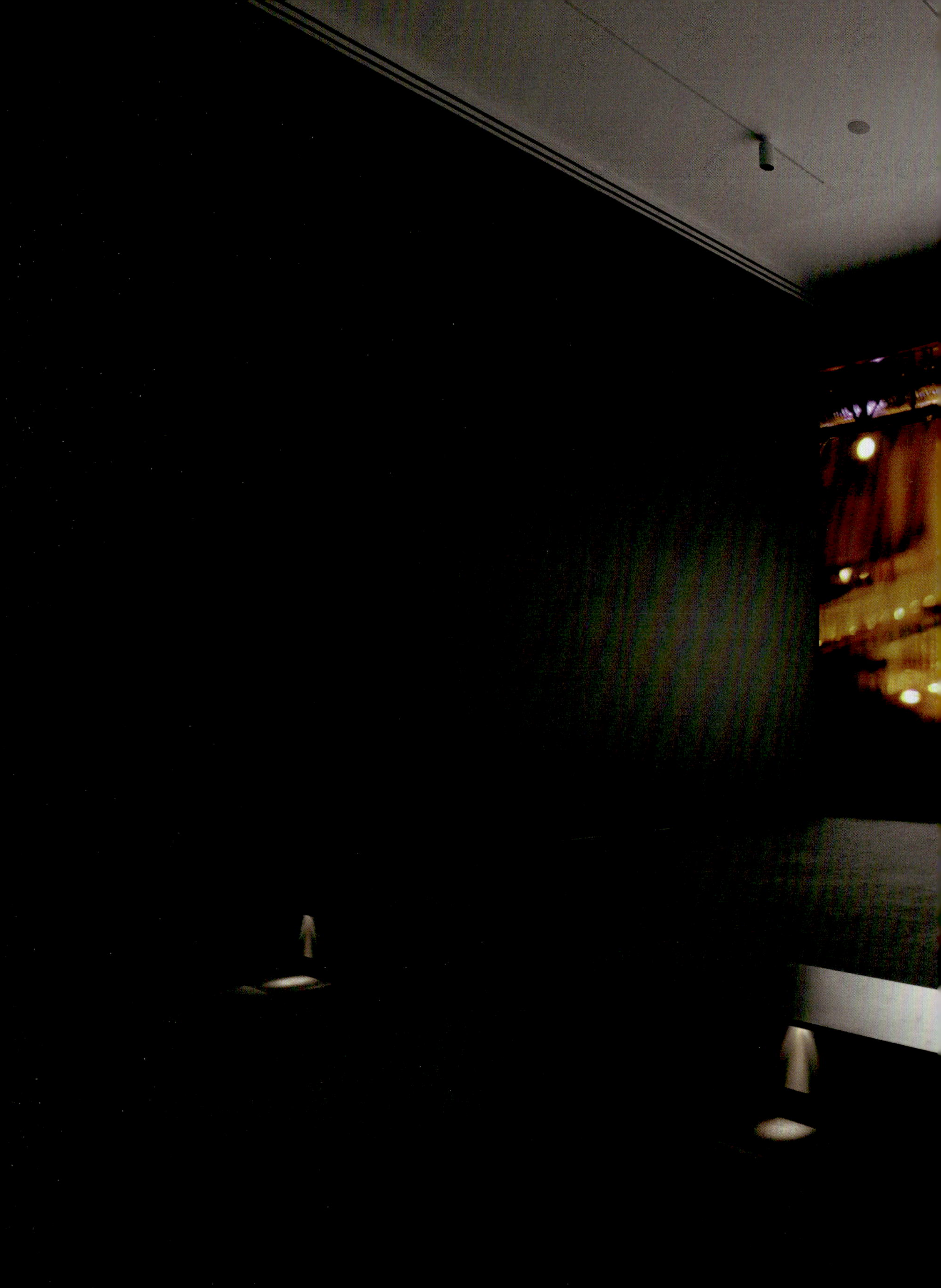

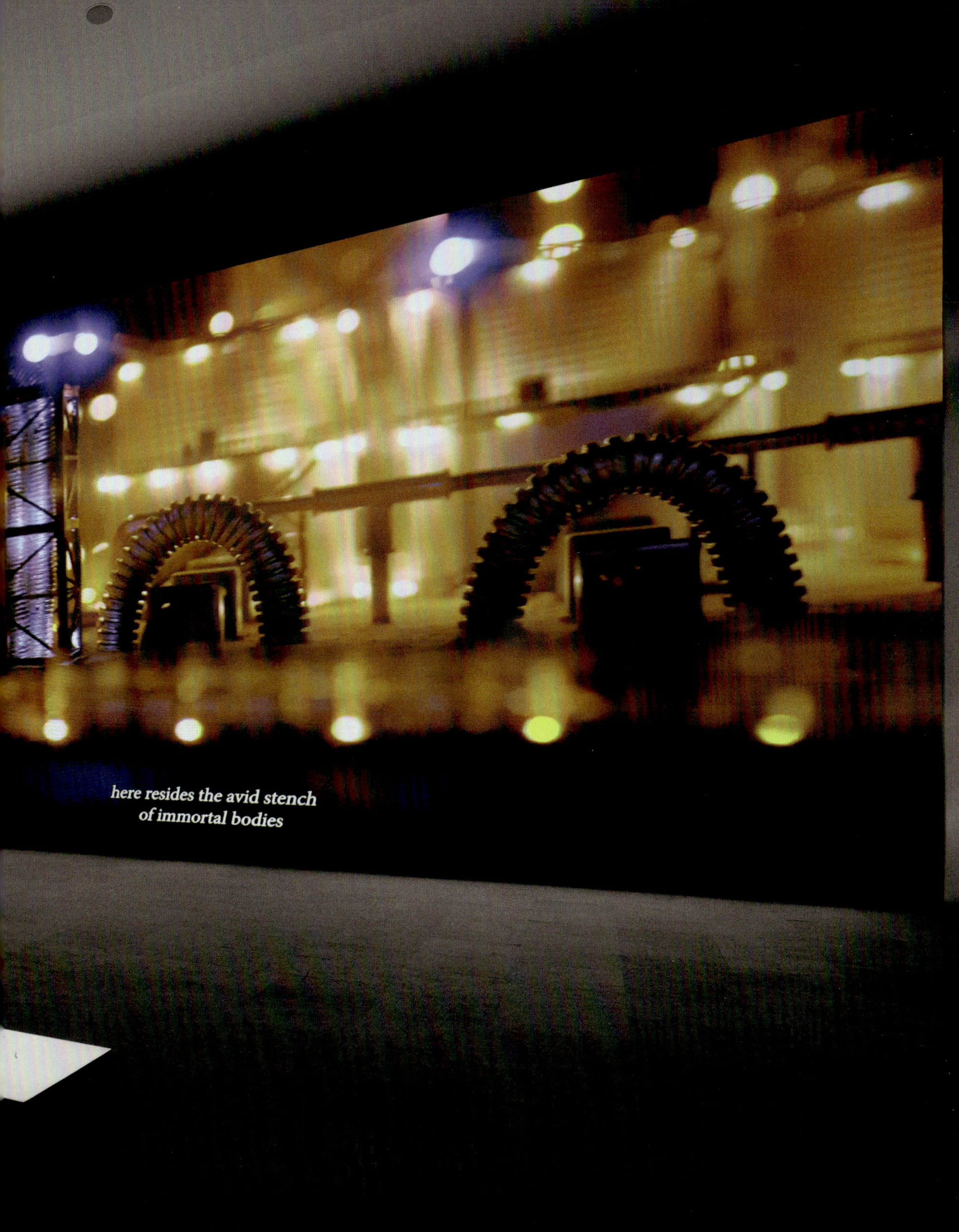
here resides the avid stench
of immortal bodies

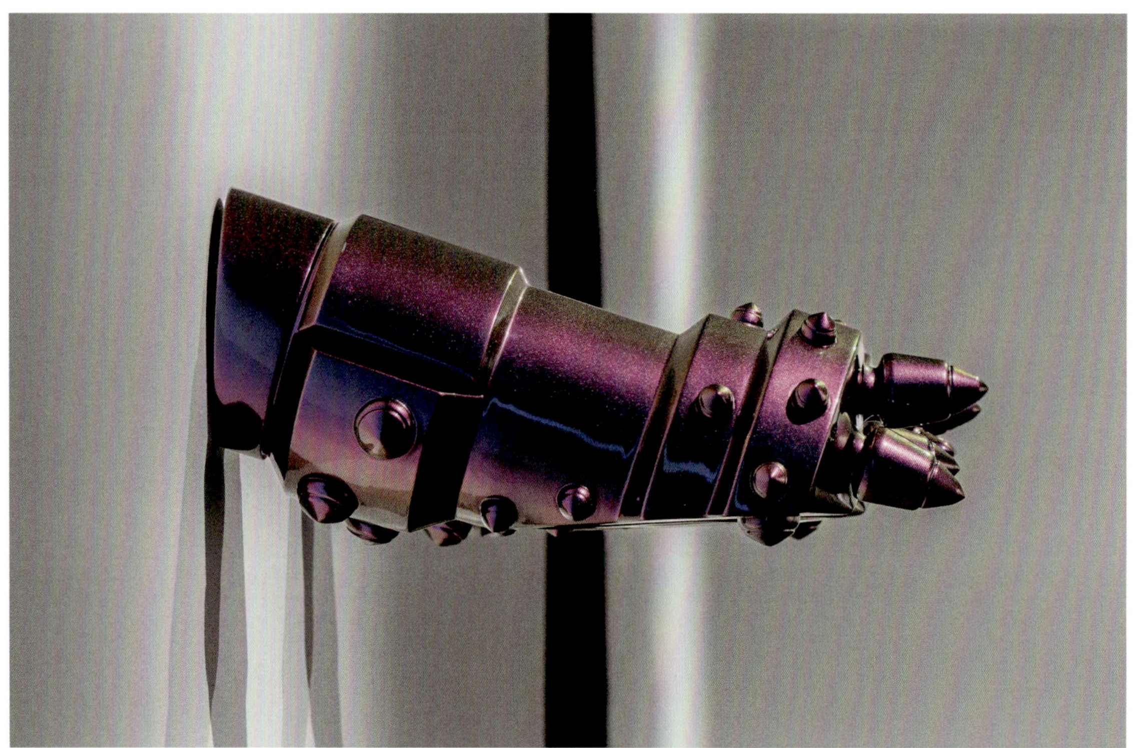

Previous spreads:
Still from *Crude Eye*,
2022. Installation
view, *Monira Al
Qadiri: Refined
Vision*, Blaffer Art
Museum. Single-
channel video,
sound; 10 minutes.

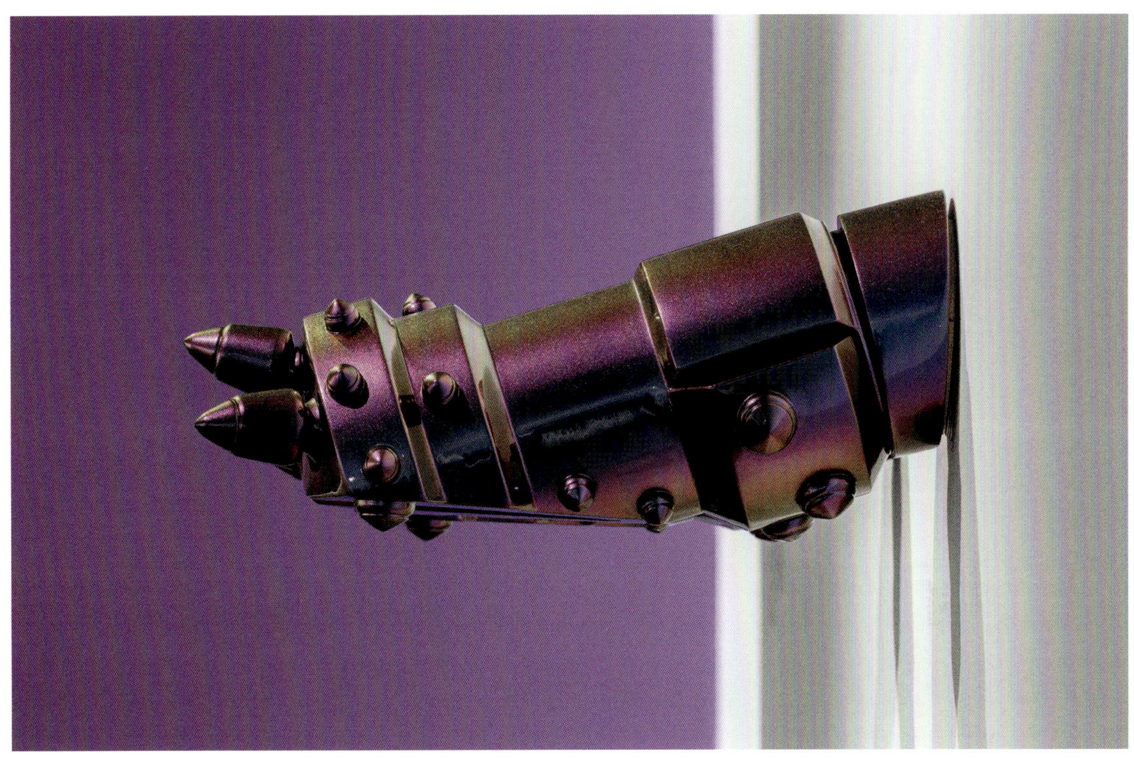

Above and opposite:
Jurassic Gauntlet, 2022 (details, installed). 3D-printed plastic, automotive paint, animatronic applications; dimensions variable.

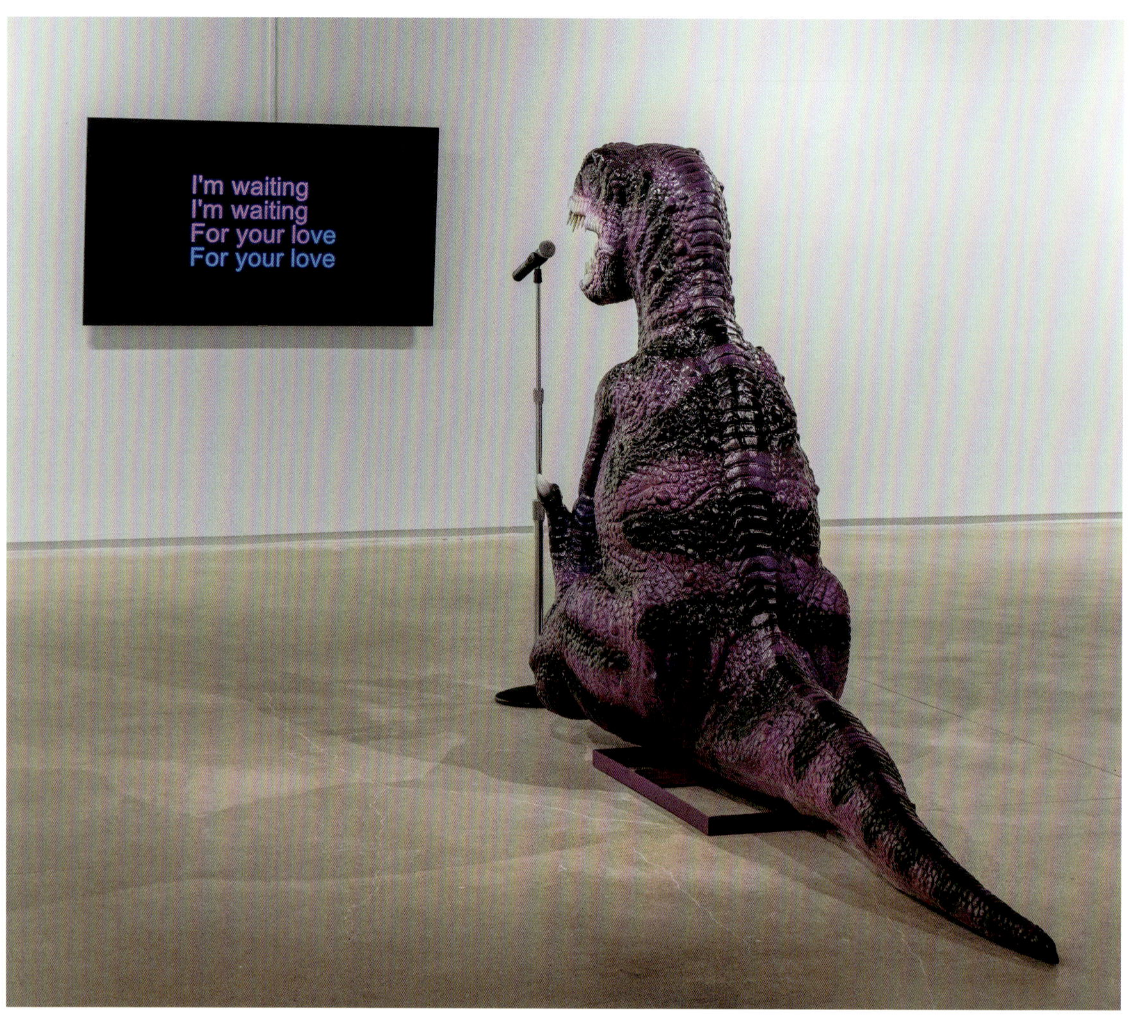

Above and opposite:
Seismic Songs,
2022. Detail and
installation view,
*Monira Al Qadiri:
Refined Vision*,
Blaffer Art Museum.
Painted silicone,
foam, microphone,
video, sound.

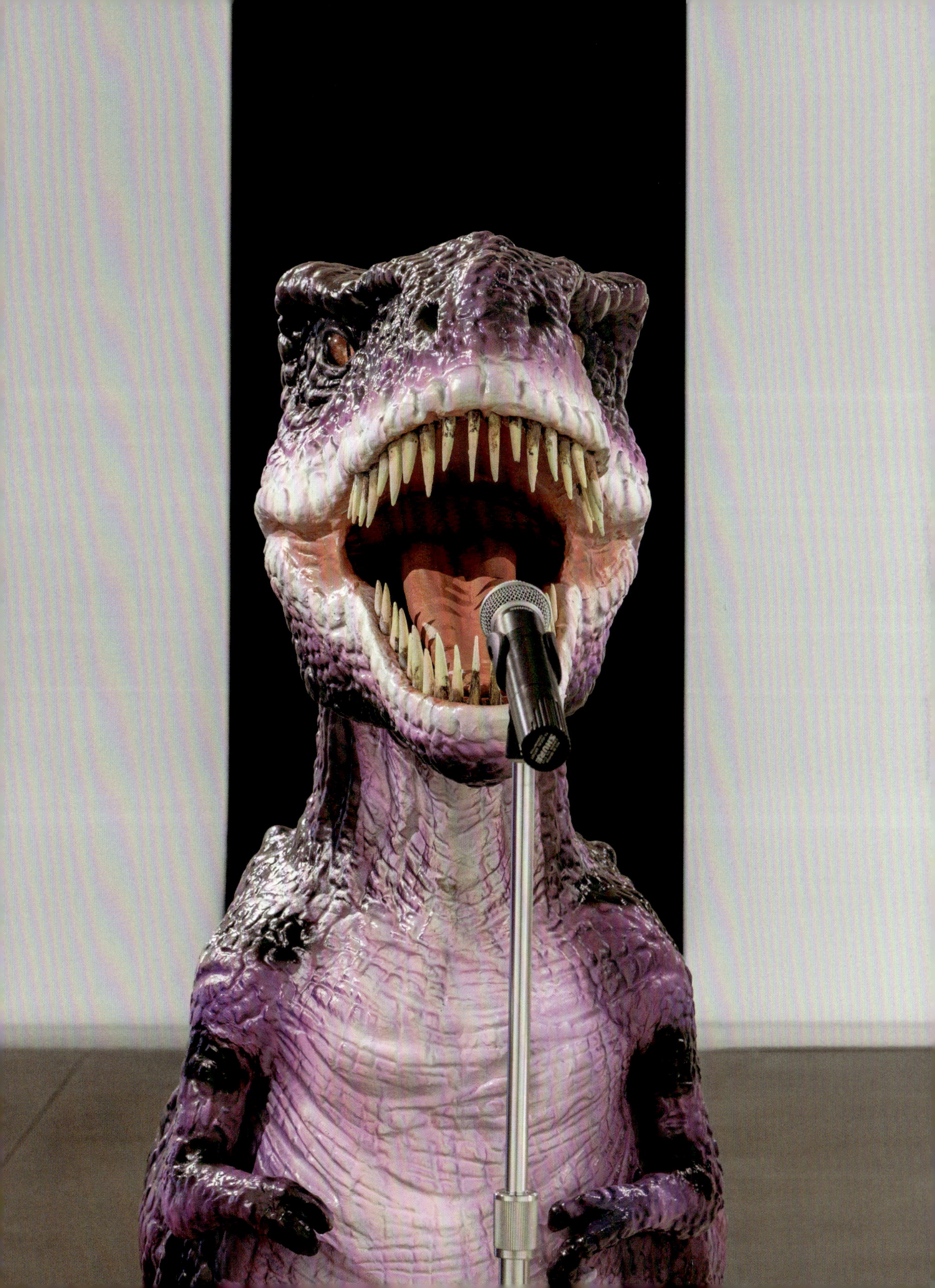

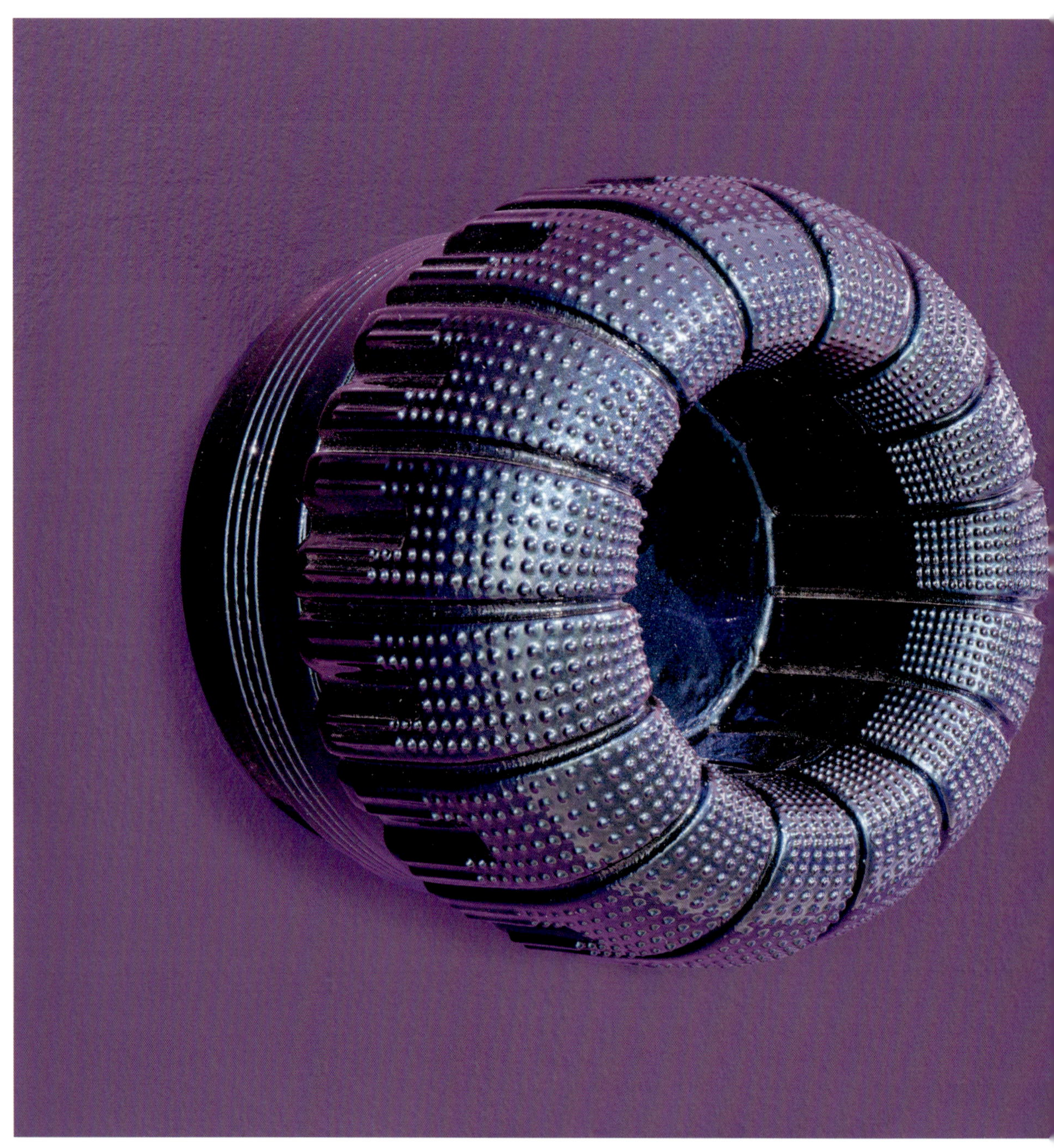

Spectrum, 2016
(detail). Six 3D-
printed sculptures,
automotive paint.

Next spread:
Installation view,
Monira Al Qadiri:
Refined Vision,
Blaffer Art Museum.

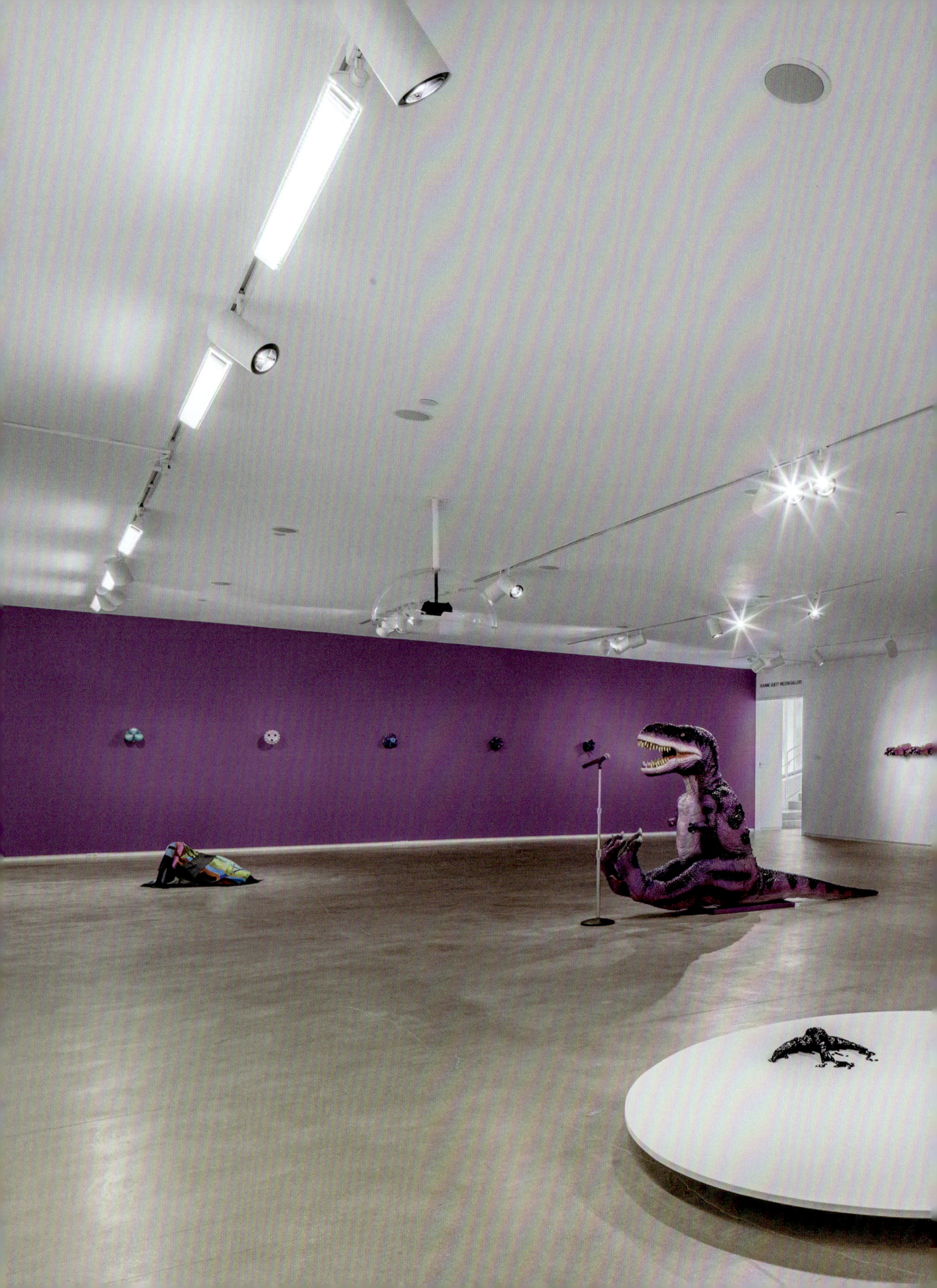

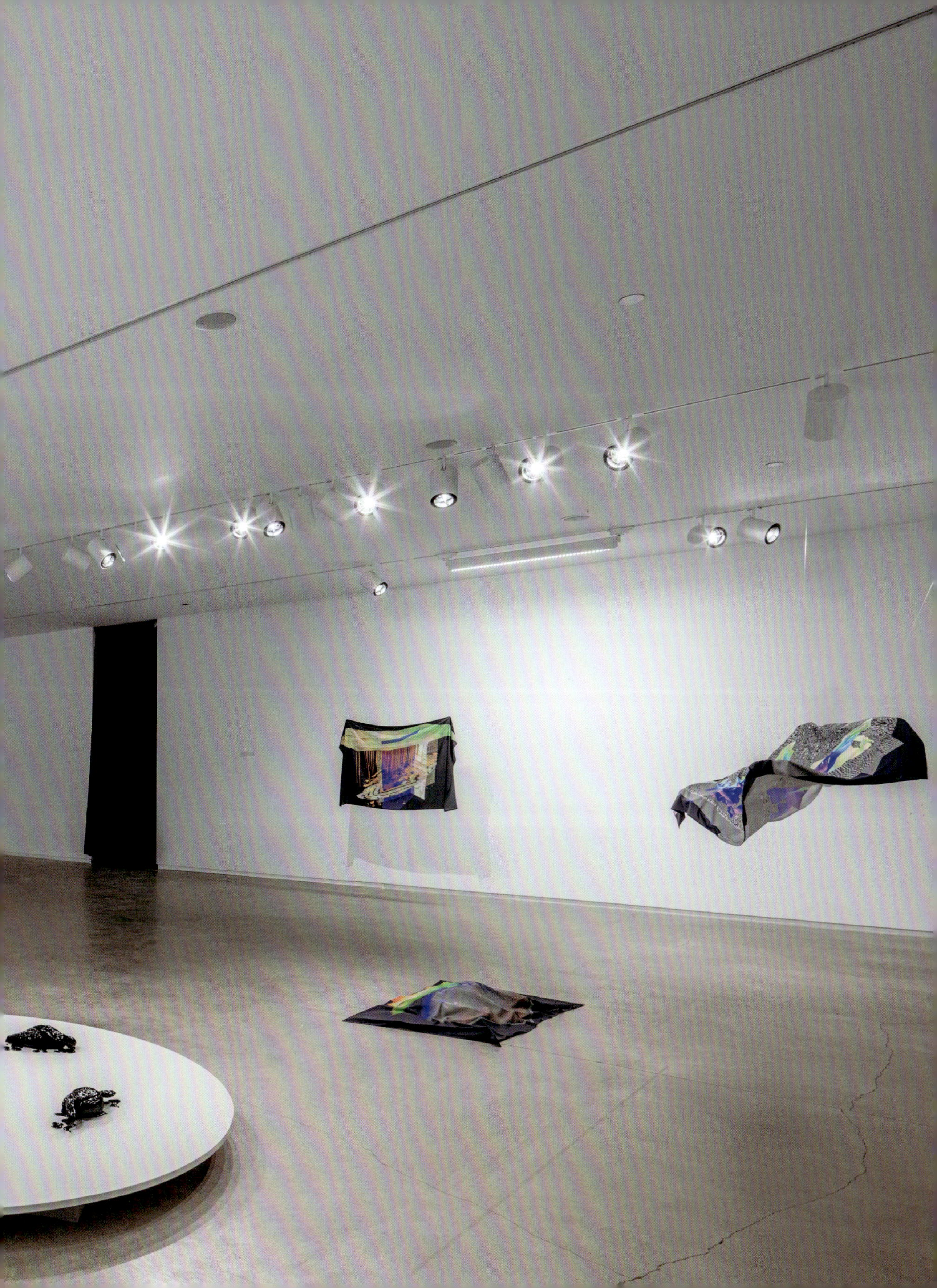

INTERVIEW WITH MONIRA AL QADIRI

Tyler Blackwell

TYLER BLACKWELL You were born in Senegal but grew up mainly in Kuwait, including during the Iraqi invasion and the first Gulf War of 1990–91. How do you think witnessing these conflicts affected your development (both personal and artistic) and your ideas about how the world works?

MONIRA AL QADIRI As a child growing up during wartime, that experience has obviously affected me immensely as a person and shaped my worldview in more ways than I'd like to admit. On the other hand, because I was only seven years old when it happened, not having a mature perception of the events in front of me also saved me from a lot of trauma later in life. But over thirty years later, I am still dealing with the aftereffects of that time. It's not something that goes away. It stays with you.

TB Is this also when you became cognizant of the value of oil and fossil fuels? Or was it later?

MAQ The first time I saw oil as a substance was during the war in Kuwait, when oil wells were burning and everything around us was coated in black, including our house, the sea, and the sky. As a child my understanding of the term "fossil fuel" was nonexistent, but those hell-like images stayed with me, and I revisited them time and time again in my work, culminating in a deeper understanding of the oil industry and attempting to tackle it through my work.

TB You have described a prevailing fascination in Kuwait with Western/American pop culture and fast food during the 1980s. Do you have

vivid memories of this sort of cultural mash-up
as a child?

MAQ Yes, so-called Americana was huge in the 1980s,
as it was in most of the developing world at the
time. There was something shiny and magical
about American pop culture; the glitz and glam
of it was blinding to us. My generation is sometimes referred to as "chicken nuggets" because
of this craze and how it affected us.

TB You moved at sixteen to Japan—a faraway nation
where you did not speak the language or know
anyone. Do you think the Gulf conflicts are what
made you want to move away as a teenager?

MAQ I think during the war I was overcome with a
desire to escape my reality, my surroundings, the
destruction I had witnessed. So, I momentarily
escaped from where I was by watching Arabic-
dubbed Japanese cartoons, which after the war
became an obsession. In an attempt to transform
myself somehow into that two-dimensional world
that I loved so much, I started teaching myself
Japanese, and I got a scholarship to study there.
I moved to Tokyo at sixteen, completely oblivi-
ous to the fact that I wasn't going to live inside a
cartoon, but that reality hit me later on.

TB How did your family react to your desire to move?

MAQ They were very encouraging, actually. My parents
had moved to Moscow to study in the '70s, then
to Africa for many years, so they were quite open
to the idea of going abroad. They were also wary
of the fact that if I remained in Kuwait, I would
learn very few life skills because of the sedentary
lifestyle subsidized by the state. They were acutely
aware of the fact that oil wealth is an illusion,
and that one had to build oneself up outside of
this comfortable environment. I think the war
also opened my parents' eyes to this reality.

TB Tell me about life in Japan.

MAQ Japan was both wonderful and very severe in equal
parts. Attending art school there was interesting, but
also highlighted for me the rigid nature of Japanese
society, and how slow they are to opening up to
new ideas and new ways of doing things. It is a very
conservative place after all. Being a foreigner there
for so long was quite taxing on me, as I always felt
like an alien, eternally out of place. But even though I
left the country behind me, I spent a significant part
of my life there, so the culture is still a part of me.

TB In Tokyo, you studied for a PhD and ended up researching the aesthetics of sadness in the Middle East that stems from poetry, music, art, and religious practice. How do you think your time in Japan influenced the way you made work?

MAQ I would say Japan has a hypervisual culture, that still influences how I approach art making today. The animated, colorful aspect of my works is a direct result of my time spent absorbing the culture there. On the other hand, I became nostalgic for the pictureless nature of Arab culture that is more focused on the literary and poetic, so I tried to mix these two worlds in my research and subsequent practice. You can say it is a hybrid viewpoint.

TB Sadness is an enduring theme in your work— it is melancholy but also, for you, generative. How do you think a legacy of cultural melancholy has charged the way you approach making works?

MAQ In many cultures around the Middle East— Arab, Iranian, Indian—sadness is seen as a noble emotion that is revered in music, poetry, art, and even religious practices. I always appreciated the richness of this emotional landscape growing up. I think I have an aversion to the modern Western clinical approach to the subject in which sadness and melancholy are viewed as symptoms of a disease that always needs to be "treated." In this way, melancholy is seen as being a state that is counterproductive to capitalist society because it hinders the productivity of the individual. The idea of revisiting this subject came to me while living in Japan, a country that is hypercapitalist as well. I felt that embedding a tragic character in my work allows it to refute the status quo somehow. It is a constant feature in my practice to this day.

TB At what point did you decide to hone in on making work about oil or "petroculture?"

MAQ After spending over a decade in Japan, I felt like a total outsider upon returning to Kuwait. I also adopted the gaze of an outsider, thinking about the massive oil wealth that existed in the region, and how it has shaped and morphed everything about that place, despite no one wanting to discuss or deal with that topic locally. Life was

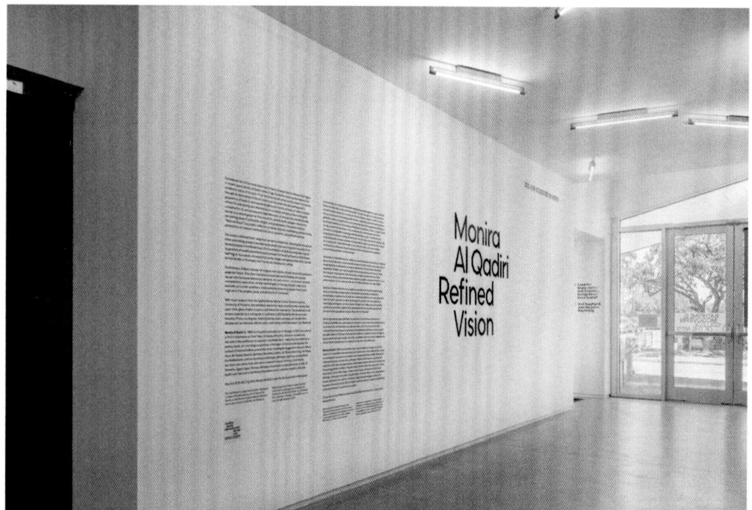

Installation view,
*Monira Al Qadiri:
Refined Vision*,
Blaffer Art Museum.

bizarre and strange to me at that specific moment: through the lens of oil, there was a certain freakish atmosphere that I saw that I couldn't unsee anymore. That's when I started addressing the concept of petroculture, as a way of illustrating that reality to myself.

TB   One of your works, *Behind the Sun*, utilizes amateur footage of burning oil fields during the Gulf conflict—a real-life hell on earth. You made this work in response to Werner Herzog's 1992 film *Lessons of Darkness*. Can you tell me a bit about your experience watching the film? *Behind the Sun* seems, in comparison, a bit like a reclamation project.

MAQ   I saw Herzog's docufiction film right after the war and I was very upset by it. Still being a child emerging from that conflict, of course I didn't understand what the docufiction genre was at all, I just had a jarring feeling: "Why is this German man lying about our war?" Even many years later, I couldn't shake this disturbance I had felt, the anger and frustration about that particular work, so I decided finally to make my own version of the film, so to speak, in order to reclaim its context for myself.

TB   *Refined Vision* is your first solo exhibition in the United States after many presentations of work across Europe and Asia. When I first wanted to work with you, I thought there might be some fascinating overlap between Houston—an American city (and in a state) made extremely wealthy from its ties to oil and gas production in the Gulf of Mexico and across the world—and the Persian Gulf region. I believe you agree. Can you tell me why you were interested in this Texas context?

MAQ   I was very attracted by the notion of exhibiting my work in Texas, as I was fascinated by the long industrial and cultural relationship Houston has cultivated with the Persian Gulf over the past century. Afterall it was mainly Texan oil men that developed the oil industry we are currently living with in Saudi Arabia, Kuwait, and elsewhere. It is a subject that has seldom been addressed in any artistic context, either in Houston itself or the Gulf region, so it felt radical and new for me to try to tackle it in this show. In a way it is a shared history, by places that are geographically extremely distant from one another.

TB   Now that you have traveled to Houston, has your perception changed? Did being in the city feel familiar?

MAQ   Sadly, my fantasy of Houston did not coincide with reality—in my mind it was a desert that was littered with oil fields, visually very much like Kuwait. But when I landed I saw the green landscape and was instantly surprised, even shocked. It's interesting to me how you can build up a vision of what a place might look like, and have that destroyed immediately. It's exhilarating actually.

TB   In the Blaffer exhibition, you explore the themes of loss, destruction, and disaster, of environmentalism, cultural history, pop culture, religion, mystery, science fiction, and more. Sometimes you do this through a humorous or surreal lens, like in the newly commissioned work *Seismic Songs* (which features a dinosaur singing karaoke), and sometimes it might be through a deeply somber work like *Onus* in which you have rendered three dead birds in sparkling black glass made to look like dripping oil. How do these methodologies coexist for you?

MAQ   As I said, I always like to inform my work with a tragic character, but the tragedy can also be so exaggerated that it becomes humorous. Over the years I have also found that humor is a weapon I can use in my work to address very serious, difficult subjects, allowing the public to digest them more easily. My works very much oscillate between these different emotional planes, and that fluctuation between concept and feeling is an important element of how I transmit my ideas.

TB Often, the "typical" American's relationship to oil and its subsequent effects on culture and the larger social psyche is seemingly less fraught than in other places like the Middle East. This I think is reflective of many things, including an isolationist mentality that has really accelerated in the last six years or so. Many of us are willfully unaware of the plights of others. In my mind your works have the subtle power to serve as a bridge for this passiveness—at least towards fossil fuels. Do you ever think of your artworks as political statements?

MAQ Even if my works are sometimes not interpreted as being overtly political on the surface, I am in fact a very political person, to a point that I don't see a separation between myself and my politics. So, the political statement is definitely there, lurking under the surface; it is just visualized in a way that can be understood in different ways by differing viewpoints. I purposely want to keep this sense of openness in my work so that I don't constrain myself to the critique itself, and that that idea or message can be transformed by other people in new and surprising ways I didn't imagine myself.

TB You are an artist who is well-versed in cultural histories, literature, and music as well as the aesthetics and strategies of advertising and communications. As a person born in Senegal, raised in Kuwait, educated in Japan, and now living in Berlin, one might describe you as truly a global citizen. You have described yourself as a "mutant." With all this in mind, how would you describe your relationship (and your practice's relationship) to language and ideas of cultural hybridity?

MAQ Sometimes I feel like a cultural Frankenstein of sorts, as I have absorbed too many cultural influences at the same time in one body. In my own case, I feel the word "hybrid" is a euphemism, something like "mutant" is more appropriate because all the parts are not always fitting

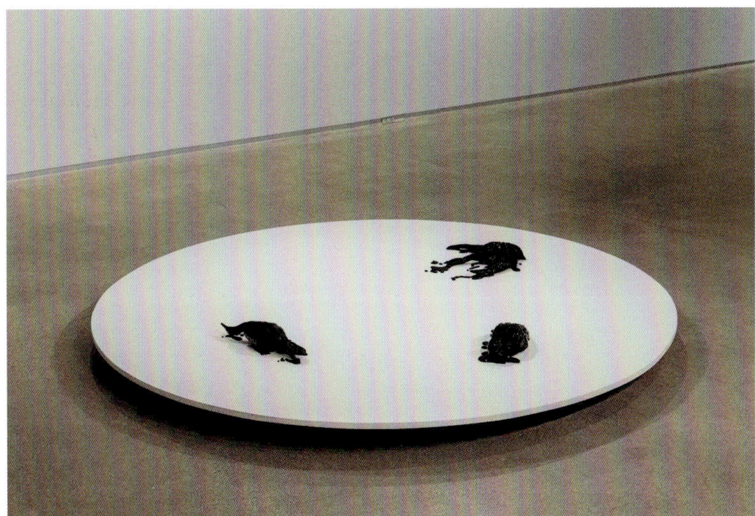

Onus, 2022.
Installation view,
*Monira Al Qadiri:
Refined Vision*,
Blaffer Art Museum.
Cast glass.

together well. They clash and oppose each other at times. This cultural tension is also visible in my work.

TB   In *Crude Eye*, a magnificent short film commissioned for this exhibition, we encounter an unnerving, alien-like voice shrouded within an ominous, electronic synth soundscape. The voice is speaking to us, telling a poetic, eerie story of a fantastical place filled with lights, phantoms, and energy. This work is inspired by your own experience as a child observing a distant oil refinery. How has time created or altered the distance you feel from these memories?

MAQ   As an adult I associate the image of the oil refinery as one of pollution, greed, and destruction because I know what it is and its effects on the natural environment around it. But as a child who has no concept of these realities, I was enamored by the *vision* of the refinery itself. I thought it was simply beautiful. The most magical, most high-tech, most mysterious cityscape that I imagined emerged from a science fiction movie or cartoon. In this film I wanted to reconcile my sense of childlike wonder of growing up next to this mysterious "city" with the knowledge I have as an adult of it being a source of destruction. In our modern world, oil plays the role of being both a miracle and a curse and many of my works try to make sense of this dilemma.

Monira Al Qadiri: Refined Vision
is published by
Inventory Press
2305 Hyperion Ave
Los Angeles, CA 90027
inventorypress.com

Blaffer Art Museum
4173 Elgin St
Houston, TX 77004

BLAFFER
ART MUSEUM
UNIVERSITY of **HOUSTON**

**Cynthia Woods
Mitchell Center
for the Arts**
UNIVERSITY OF **HOUSTON**

© 2024 Inventory Press, Los Angeles; Blaffer Art
Museum, Houston, TX; and the authors.

Copyediting and Proofreading
Eugenia Bell

Design
IN-FO.CO
(Adam Michaels, V. E. Chen, Ásta Þrastardóttir,
Marina Kitchen)

Printed and bound in Belgium by die Keure

ISBN: 978-1-941753-60-6
LCCN: 2024933769

Distributed by
ARTBOOK | D.A.P.
75 Broad St, Suite 630
New York, NY 10004
artbook.com

Photography Credits
All images courtesy Blaffer Art Museum, University
of Houston; photographed by Francisco Ramos unless
otherwise noted.

pp. 14, 17, 19: Courtesy the artist.

pp. 8, 37, 50: Commissioned by Blaffer Art Museum and
the Cynthia Woods Mitchell Center for the Arts.

Cover and back cover: *Jurassic Gauntlet*, 2022 (detail).
3D-printed plastic, automotive paint, animatronic applications. Commissioned by Blaffer Art Museum and the
Cynthia Woods Mitchell Center for the Arts.

Endpapers: Still from *Crude Eye*, 2022. Single-channel
video, sound; 10 minutes. Commissioned by Blaffer Art
Museum and the Cynthia Woods Mitchell Center for the
Arts. Miniature model: Anika Klatt; cinematography:
Karam Ghoussein; editing: Vartan Avakian; music:
Fatima Al Qadiri; sound design: James Kelly; coloring:
Chrystel Elias.